Matrixing Kenpo Karate

BOOK ONE

The Real History

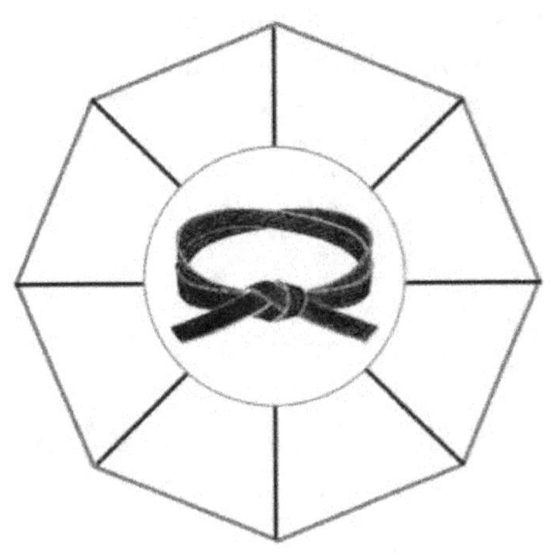

Al Case

Quality Press

Copyright © 2024 by Alton H. Case

Formerly titled 'How to Create Kenpo Karate'

For more information go to:

MonsterMartialArts.com

Table of Contents

introduction 5
The History of Kenpo 7
James Mitose 9
Thunderbolt Chow 12
Ed Parker 13
The Tracy Brothers 16
Rod Martin 18
Al Case 20
Kang Duk Won 22
What's Wrong with Kenpo (pt 1) 26
Matrixing 28
What's Wrong with Kenpo (pat 2) 31
Matrixing Motion in Kenpo 33
Conclusion to the History 34
A List of Kenpo Techniques 36
Orange Belt Techniques 43
Purple Belt Techniques 102
About the Author 124

Introduction

There is a school of thought, in the martial arts, that to be good one must do as they are told, must memorize long and laborious forms, must memorize endless strings of random techniques.

Kenpo is one of these schools, and, I hate to say it, perhaps the worst. There are hundreds of random strings of moves to memorize, the forms are more for dance than creating power, and freestyle is a thing apart.

And, sad to say, nobody objects, they treat the art as if sacred, never to be questioned.

Yet, if you examine those who brought it to us, they questioned the heck out of it.

Mitose was interested in self defense techniques, Chow was interested in street fighting techniques, and Parker...Parker was interested in creating a lasting ode to himself.

So we are left with something that worked for them, but which has become a mish mash to us.

The purpose of these three books, 'Matrixing Kenpo,' is to cause you, the student, to question.

To question the masters, to question the system, to question yourselves.

To do this, to raise these questions, we will examine Kenpo using something called Matrixing.

Matrixing is a form of logic.

What matrixing does is enable the student to see a martial art with such clarity that he or she can tailor that art to his or her own specific lights; in this case, to create kenpo so that it is not a series of memorized techniques, but rather a creation of the self.

To reach this point, where you create the art, is the essence of all arts, it is the mark of the true artist.

Matrixing Kenpo Karate consists of three volumes.

The first volume has the history, including the mistakes of the pioneers, and the analysis of 54 Kenpo techniques.

The second volume continues with the analysis of techniques, and includes a short section on how to revise and recreate the forms of Kenpo.

The third volume concludes the analysis of techniques, then presents a complete revision of Kenpo, including all belts, and the matrixing theory behind this. You will learn how to write a matrix of your own at this point, though for complete information on how to make and use matrixes you are recommended to view the series called 'Matrixing Karate.'

Now, enjoy, and have a great work out!

Al Case

The History of Kenpo

Kenpo means 'Fist Law.' It is derived from 'chuan fa.'

The fame of kenpo, is often attributed to Ed Parker.

Ed Parker popularized the art, was at the forefront of the martial arts invasion of the United States, and thus the world.

The Ed Parker story, however, is only the tip of the iceberg.

Right behind Ed Parker loom several very large figures., including Thunderbolt Chow and James Mitose.

And, after Parker, there are a host of Kenpo practitioners, genius in their own rights.

And that brings us to Matrixing.

Matrixing is a simple subject, but large. We will be going into the concepts as we proceed with this book.

For now, however, let's just point out that Matrixing is the first and only science of the martial arts. It resurrects lost arts, fixes corrupted arts, and returns the martial arts to a method that is enlightening to all mankind.

In applying Matrixing to Kenpo we come up with many problems.

To understand these problems, however, we must not merely list them, or point them out righteously, but rather we must delve into and assume a viewpoint of history that will enable you to understand the significance of matrixing, what was done to the martial arts, and, in specific, to Kenpo.

By pointing out what actually went wrong we will be in a better position to fix Kenpo.

Having said that, I am full aware that I will have my detractors. There will be those that cling to corruption, hold distraction as truth, and refuse to consider matrixing as valid.

But history is history, and matrixing is a science, so consider my words, and work the techniques. In the techniques is the truth of the art, and of yourself.

And remember that the things you will be learning, the concepts that will be permeating your soul, are likely the very things that the founders of yesterday went through in putting Kenpo together.

Maybe you will reach the same conclusions as they. Maybe not. While the truth is always the same, the various viewpoints of that truth can vary wildly.

The point, however, is that when the instructors of yesterday learned the martial arts, the martial arts were not well known. Indeed, to learn the martial arts as little as fifty years ago was to experience something with little relative history, not much in the way of background, and very little roots.

It was pure, and it was writ upon the students purely, with no distraction, and relatively little corruption.

Now there is corruption and distraction aplenty.

Tournaments. MMA. Protective gear. Making money through contracts. Etcetera.

These are things that didn't exist, or were not of much significance, when people were learning the martial arts only a few decades ago.

So prepare yourself.

Put yourself in a zen state of mind.

E tabulas rasa.

Prepare to be written on.

For the truth treats all distraction and corruption as nothing.

James Mitose

James Masayoshi Mitose was born on December 30, 1916. He was born in Hawaii, but his family returned to Japan when he was four years old.

He received a thorough education in Japan, including a study of Martial Arts. These martial arts included what appears to be Okinawan Karate and Japanese Jujitsu. Mr. Mitose has stated that his martial arts were Japanese, and not Okinawan, the style of Karate he studied, however, seems to be Okinawan in nature.

Mr. Mitose says he studied martial arts at the Shaka-In temple, near the town of Misato. This temple would have been where the Kosho sect of the Yoshida clan had their existence.

When James was 21 years old he returned to Hawaii and began teaching the martial arts.

It was 1936 when he first began teaching, and he opened his first school in 1941. This was likely the first martial arts school in the United States. This was prior to Hawaii becoming a state, however, so there is some argument concerning this fact.

During his lifetime Mr. Mitose used several names to describe his teaching. Among the names are:

Shorinji Kempo
Kempo Jujitsu
Kosho Shorei-ryu

The word Kenpo (Kempo) is Japanese translation of 'Chuan Fa.' Chuan Fa is Chinese for 'fist principles,' or 'Way of the Fist,' or 'Fist Law.'

When world War 2 broke out Mitose signed up with the national guard, but was discharged shortly, and then sent to an internment camp.

He was released from internment in 1942 and spent the war years teaching Kenpo to prepare people for a possible Japanese invasion of the islands.

Interesting to note, Mr. Mitose also worked as an herbalist, and gained a good reputation as a healer.

Odd to note, he also owned a brothel.

James would arrive several books on the martial arts. These books, while discussing such things as Tai Sabaki principles, reveal his art to be heavily influenced by Okinawan arts. One of the books, 'What is Self Defense?, duplicates an earlier book written by Okinawan Karate pioneer Higaonna Kamesuke. This includes diagrams and images.

Because of these facts, and Mitose's own words, his main teacher, or lineage, seems to be from Motobu Choki.

An interesting side note here, in the early 1920s Karate was just becoming known in Japan. One master of Karate was Motobu Choki.

One night he went to a fighting competition, and the main fighter, a Russian, or at least a westerner, offered a challenge. Motobu answered the challenge, and knocked the Russian out quickly.

Writers from the newspapers were excited by this, and quickly sent in their stories. Unfortunately, they had no pictures of Motobu, and so the editors selected a picture at random of young Gichin Funakoshi. Thus, Mr. Funakoshi received all the credit, and became famous and and provided the main impetus for the expansion of his system of Karate around the world.

Yet it was Motobu, and his style, that provided the knock out.

At any rate, Mr. Mitose taught in the manner of the old school (of Motobu), which is to say very few Kata (Naihanchi seems to have been his only Kata), and heavy practice of techniques.

The final name for Mr. Mitose's system was Kosho Shorei-Ryu Kenpo, which means 'Old Pine Tree School of Encouragement.'

In the 1950s Mitose moved to California and began teaching Martial Arts in Los Angeles. One of his students was a fellow name of Terry Lee, who took on the name of Nimr Hassan. He taught Terry for about one year.

In 1974 Hassan was arrested for blackmail and murder, having threatened, and then murdered, by stabbing and strangulation and other brutalities, a Mr. Namimatsu.

Hassan claimed that Mitose had told him to commit the murder, and even provided the means (rope and knife?) to do so.

Mr. Mitose was arrested. The trial was lacking in competence, as adequate translators were not provided for Mr. Mitose.

In the end, Mitose took full responsibility, and this because Hassan was his student.

That it was Terry Lee that committed the murder is proven, by evidence and his own words. He claimed that, though the injuries he had delivered to Mr. Namimatsu resulted in his death, Mr. Namimatsu was still alive when he left the scene of the crime, so he was not guilty.

At any rate, Mr. Mitose went to prison, where he died eight years later due to complications from diabetes.

Hassan, who actually committed the murder, because he turned state's evidence (accused his teacher) only received three years in prison. When released he began teaching the martial arts, claiming that he was the rightful heir to Mitose's system.

Thus, one of the most important men in the history of the Martial Arts, and certainly Kenpo, was poorly treated.

His students include William Chow, Bruce Juchnik, Ray Arquilla, Arthur Keawe, Edward "Bobby" Lowe, Giro Nakamura, Grandmaster Fusae Oshita (sister), Paul Yamaguchi, Thomas S.H. Young, Ray Arquilla.

William 'Thunderbolt' Chow

William Kwai Sun Chow was born in Hawaii on July 3rd, 1914.

Initially, Chow was taught by his father, who might have been a buddhist priest.

When his father returned to China, Chow studied boxing, wrestling, jujitsu and karate. He was particularly interested in street techniques.

Eventually, he studied under James Mitose, becoming one of only five black belts awarded by Mr. Mitose.

Chow was short, only 5' 2", and he tested his techniques on the streets of Hawaii, especially enjoying taking on military MPs.

In 1944 Chow began teaching Kenpo Karate at a YMCA in Honolulu. He never actually had a dojo, but preferred teaching in parks. He didn't teach kata, and only taught techniques. He was known for focusing specifically on street techniques.

Because he was extremely explosive in the application of his techniques he gained the nickname 'Thunderbolt.'

His students include such people as:
Ed Parker, Adriano Emperado, Paul Yamaguchi, Abe Kamahoahoa, Bobby Lowe, Ralph Castro, Sam Kuoha, John Leone, William G. Marciarelli, Paul Pung, Ron Alo,

Ed Parker

We come now to the father of American Kenpo, Edmund Kealoha Parker.

I am going to be saying some things here that people may not like, and that people might disagree with. So be it. The lessons of history are not learned by closing one eye. One must look at the bad as well as the good, consider all the factors, and not judge somebody for making the decisions he made. After all, walk a mile in his shoes...

Ed was born on March 19, 1931.

He earned a black belt in Judo by the time he was 18. He was also interested in boxing. In the 1940s he was introduced to William Chow, and earned a brown belt in Kenpo Karate from him.

Ed went to the mainland to Brigham Young University. At the university he taught classes in Kenpo Karate. Later, he moved to Los Angeles and opened a Kenpo Karate school.

The story goes that he taught people up to brown belt, then ran out of material to teach. So he went home to Hawaii and tried to get more material from Thunderbolt Chow, but Mr. Chow refused to teach him more because he had been teaching without permission.

At the time, the martial arts were just beginning to grow, and Ed was rubbing elbows with some very knowledgeable people. This included such martial artists as Ark Wong, Haumea Lefiti, James Wing Woo, and Lau Bun.

These people taught a wide variety of martial arts, including San Soo, Tai Chi, Hung Gar and Splashing Hands.

That Ed was influenced by these relationships is obvious, as principles of these arts would later appear in the Kenpo that Ed taught.

Searching for more material to teach his students, Ed became friends with James (Jimmy) Wing Woo.

Woo was a VERY good martial artist, and he became involved with Ed in the writing of a martial arts book.

Jimmy moved in with Ed and even taught Ed's classes in Pasadena.

Eventually, the book was done, and the story goes that Jimmy saw a copy of the book and asked why his name wasn't on it.

'Let's take a ride, Jimmy," Ed is supposed to have said.

They went for a ride, and Ed dropped Jimmy off in Hollywood and drove away.

Jimmy didn't speak English well, and had only one quarter in his pocket. He used that quarter to call one of Ed's black belts and ask for help.

The end result of this was that Jimmy opened up his own Kung Fu school in Hollywood, and all of Ed's upper belts, except for two brown belts left Ed for Jimmy.

Now, how much of this is true? After all, it is a scurrilous story which paints Ed in a rather poor light.

For an answer one is recommended to the website of Jimmy Woo. As of this writing he is in his 80s and still teaching in Hollywood.

Jimmy merely states that there was a disagreement over the publishing of the book, and that he moved on.

Having noted the above, it is time to delve into the history of Kenpo from a technical viewpoint.

Ed learned Kenpo Karate, which apparently had no forms. He probably taught strict Okinawan style techniques. If you look at one of the books Ed wrote it shows the techniques in order, and they look exactly like the Heian forms of Japanese Karate.

Running out of material, regardless of the circumstances, Ed tapped into the genius of Jimmy Woo. This is likely where Kenpo picked up a large number of forms, and where Kenpo began taking on a decidedly Kung Fu slant.

In total, there are supposed to have been five versions of Kenpo.

In all honesty, this author can't be totally sure which version he learned.

And, in truth, it likely doesn't matter, considering the scope of this book.

Whether one learned version 1 or version 5, Matrixing is still going to have its effect, and provide a viewpoint for understanding the truth of Kenpo.

Past this technical viewpoint, returning to the history of Ed Parker, there are other rumors, some kind, some nasty.

But rumors don't matter, and the ones relayed here are merely to give a better understanding not just of the man, but of what kinds of things he had to confront to spread Kenpo.

So let's look at what Edmund Parker, brown belt, actually did.

Ed opened one of the first Kenpo Karate schools in America.

He publicized it through movies and friendships with such celebrities as Elvis Presley.

He taught legitimate grandmasters of some magnitude, including such people as Mills Crenshaw, Tom Garriga, Rick Flores, Al and Jim Tracy, Chuck Sullivan, John McSweeney, and Dave Hebler.

He promoted the 'Internationals,' one of the largest and most prestigious tournaments and demos of its time.

He was friends with Bruce Lee, giving Bruce a helping hand by featuring him at the Internationals. He even pointed Danny Inosanto to Bruce.

He publicized Kenpo with a minor career as a stuntman and actor.

He taught and aided Jeff Speakman in his movie career.

He wrote many books.

He influenced the martial arts, not just Kenpo, forever.

So, did he do bad things? Probably.

Does the good outweigh the bad? Definitely.

And, in the long view, even if people don't like Edmund Parker, the truth is in his art. Kenpo is his legacy, and any can learn that magnificent art, they can benefit from Ed Parker's teachings whether they like him or not.

That's a pretty good legacy.

The Tracy Brothers

Two of Parker's students were Al and Jim Tracy. They began studied with Parker in 1957, and opened their first Kenpo Karate school in San Francisco in 1962.

A third brother, Will, studied under William Chow, receiving his black belt in 1961.

The Tracy's were lawyers, but decided that Kenpo Karate was the wave of the future, and determined to be in on it.

One fact of note: Ed Parker changed his system of Kenpo in 1962, calling it Chinese Kenpo. The Tracy Brothers stayed with the older system of Kenpo, as taught by Mitose and Chow.

The Tracy brothers set about bringing the teaching of Karate into modern times.

First, they revamped the belt system, introducing a plethora of colors. The result of this was that students had more incentive and worked harder.

They also created three new 'kyu' ranks. Kyu ranks are the lower more colorful belts.

They sorted the techniques into groups of forty (for each belt).

They also gave more colorful names to the techniques, which added to the mystique and made the techniques easier to remember. Interestingly, Parker rejected the belt system for several years.

One of the more significant changes they made was the introduction of contracts; the Tracy's apparently hired a car salesman to formulate contracts such as the ones used to buy cars. This particular item has been partially responsible the term 'McDojo,' and caused many martial artists to speak ill of the Tracy's.

For years, this author went along with the general bad mouthing, then realized something: if it wasn't for contracts he might not have signed up, and might not have stuck with it in the beginning.

So, are contracts bad?

History teaches us that new ideas are not spread by themselves, but follow along the path of merchants.

And, in the final light, consider that people who speak ill of other people are less than adequate themselves. If they were integrated people they would be helping mankind, not speaking ill of it.

Thus, the people who speak ill of the Tracy's are usually those who have failed to make money teaching Karate, or, are at the least envious of the Tracy's great success.

And it is success.

The Tracy's have remained true to their roots, have built the largest martial arts chain in the world, spread the teachings of Kenpo wildly, and have been at the heart of a vast martial arts explosion.

Having said that, while this author is not sure which of the Kenpo variations he has learned, there is evidence that it is the true art of Kenpo as taught by Chow and Mitose; he learned from one of the students of the Tracy's.

To continue, the Tracy's eventually split from Parker. Mr. Parker had put the Tracy's in charge of his organization, and then decided to change everything, and the Tracy's wouldn't go along with the changes.

So they split, and Parker would then say that he didn't teach the Tracy's all his techniques, but that he had taught everything to Jeff Speakman.

What he said doesn't ring true, and is moot in light of the fact that Will Tracy studied under Chow.

Rod Martin

So, we have a strange mix occurring. Parker earned his brown belt, changed his system five times, and told the world the Tracy Brothers were only brown belts.

Then, the Tracy's hold that Parker has been untrue to the teachings, and they go to (choke) car contracts.

And, out of this mix comes Rod Martin.

Rod was a slight fellow of tremendous martial ability.

He felt that he was passed over, that he should have been promoted to black belt, and so went his own way.

Well, Parker went his own way, and the Tracy's went their own way, and...why shouldn't Martin go his own way?

He opened his Kenpo Karate school in Mountain View California.

He quickly built the school into great success, which included the making of this writer into one of his instructors.

Things were happening so fast back then, and before anybody knew it, he had several schools.

And then he created his own association, and I got to travel to tournaments and to other schools and compare myself to others, to fight and to learn.

It was great times back then, and we lived for freestyle, to learn the newest mystical technique, and we thought ourselves unbeatable.

And, I kept a notebook of techniques.

One day I was walking through the school and I passed a another instructor immersed in a three ring binder. Didn't even look up as I passed.

Then another one.

And, in the instructor's area, I saw another one.

"Hey," I asked. "Whacha got?"

He handed me the binder.

It was all my notes.

Apparently Rod had seen my notebook on a chair, and he copied it and shared it.

Now, tell the truth, I thought that was pretty cool.

And, it was the first book I wrote.

In retrospect, these many years later, it is terrible. And the proof is that I had so much trouble figuring out my own writing when I put together this book.

Still, we all start somewhere, and maybe if I hadn't put that book together, maybe I wouldn't have written later books.

Nah. I would have written them.

But it did help to have that shot in the arm way back then. Everybody likes to be recognized.

Special note: My particular instructor was a fellow named Rex. I believe his last name was Blaine, though I do apologize if memory has failed me.

Rex was one of the nicest people I have ever met, and a definite influence. His favorite trick was to place a brick on a fence, unsupported,and then shatter it with a snapping panther fist, or 'half fist.'

Al Case

Which brings us to...me.

No more of the grammatically accepted term 'this writer.'

Let me give you a short history of myself, which will segue into how I discovered matrixing.

I walked into Rod Martin's Kenpo Karate Dojo in November of 1967. I actually had no intention of signing up for instruction, but was only there with a friend who did intend to sign up.

But, courtesy of a car contract and some VERY nice people, I did sign up. Five lessons for $20.

The first lesson, I had no idea what I was doing, thought it was a lark, and just grinned at all the rigamarole and names and things.

The second lesson it was still funny, but not so funny, and I started looking around, looking for whatever this odd feeling I had was.

The third lesson I was listening to the instructor, and suddenly the room glowed golden. I remember staring at the clock, and knowing that time didn't exist, that I was in between those things called seconds.

I looked at the dust, suspended in the air, glowing golden.

And I had the thought:

I'm going to do this for the rest of my life.

And the lesson continued.

As I said earlier, I was obsessed. I learned the techniques, practiced them, wrote them down, and practiced some more.
I was especially enamored of freestyle. I found it the most exciting game in the world.

And, I became an instructor. And I was sure there was no more exalted position in the history of the universe.

Then something happened.

I was working at a place called the 'Red Barn.' It was a chicken and hamburger fast food franchise down the street from the karate school.

I was the night manager, and I had lots of kids under my direction. And, let me tell you, this was a direct result of the way I had been treated at the Kenpo school, of becoming an instructor, of finding out what I wanted to do with my life.

One night I was watching a fellow work. He was sort of a jerk, I didn't like him, but, my job was not to like, it was to get the chicken cooked and the hamburgers flipped.

Suddenly, this dweeb, this jerk, gave a hop and kicked the wall.

The wall shook, dust from the rafters. And my eyes opened.

I quickly grabbed the nerd by the arm, "What did you do? What is that" The answer: Karate.

But it was not Karate like I had ever seen. This was sheer, raw power.

So I became friends with a dweeb, and he took me to meet his brother, who knew more Karate then him and could explain his system better.

His brother turned out to be a Hell's Angel.

And, I got myself thrown through a wall. A couple of times, and became a convert.

Now, this story is told, in entirety, in 'The Neutronic Viewpoint,' and I recommend that book for the full story.

Right now, let's just consider that I had a problem.

I wanted to study this thing I had learned about, this art called Kang Duk Won. But I was an instructor at Rod Martin's Kenpo Karate school.

But, just as when the student is ready the Master will appear, a solution also appeared.

I was drafted.

And, I decided I didn't want to go to Vietnam and kill people. I wanted to learn Karate.

So I left the army, and instead of going back to Rod Martin's, I went to the Kang Duk Won in San Jose.

I began learning classical Karate under the instruction of Robert J. Babich. Bob. And, as the saying goes, the world would never be the same.

I know I am giving quite a bit of material here, and it is badly abbreviated, but let me offer one more section on my history before we go into what is wrong with Kenpo, Matrixing, and how to fix Kenpo.

Let me give a short history of the Kang Duk Won.

Kang Duk Won

In the 1930s there was a young Korean named Yoon Byung In.

Yoon wanted to study martial arts in the worst way, but the only instructor around was Chinese, and Koreans weren't accepted.

Yoon asked,then he peeked in the windows at the classes, but was always run off.

Finally, he began lining up the students' shoes on the porch while they were in class. The Kung Fu master was much impressed, and decided to accept the young Korean for instruction.

A note: the kung fu master taught Chuan Fa, which, as we know from earlier reading in this book, means 'Fist Law.'

Yoon studied hard, and proved to be a bright student.

Eventually, his family tapped him for higher education, and he traveled to a distant university.

At the university there was a karate class, and one day a Korean was running away from the Japanese karate students.

Apparently, he had signed up for karate class, then decided a girlfriend was more important, and now the karate students were determined to teach him the error of his ways.

The student ran up to Yoon and appealed for protection.

Yoon provided that protection, and managed to fight off the entire pack of students...without striking or otherwise harming any of them.

The karate master who taught the students heard the tale, and went to meet the young Korean who presented himself so well.

The karate master's name was Kanken Toyama.

And, Toyama and Yoon decided to trade systems.

Yoon quickly became an instructor, and was promoted to fourth black belt.

Eventually, Yoon returned to Korea, where he began teaching Karate.

And, there is much evidence that Yoon was at the heart of the original five Kwans.

Then the Korean war started.

These were times when only the most dedicated studied. These students would practice karate while shells were literally dropping a hundred yards away.

If the shelling got close, they would pick up the boards of the floor and move on.

The boards were never nailed down because the students knew the dojo might have to move.

Imagine doing your jump spinning kicks on boards that have become splintered and broken from constant moving. Imagine picking out a spike of wood from your foot, then continuing your practice, ignoring the bloody footprints of your forms and techniques.

Yoon's brother was an officer in the north, and he came home and demanded that Yoon go north with him.

Yoon fought, and was eventually captured and held prisoner on an island off the coast of Korea.

When the war ended, and amnesty was granted to the prisoners, Yoon was dogpiled and prevented from going home to the south.

Yoon taught Karate briefly in the north, after the war, but the communists apparently didn't like his system. This writer can only surmise that a method that created individuals with initiative was against the grain of communist principles.

Yoon was forced to work in a cement factory, where he eventually contracted cancer.

Thus, one of the greatest martial artists of the world returned home, broken and penniless, to die.

But, the worth of a man's life is determined by his work. And Yoon's real work was in the establishment of Karate in Korea.

The five kwans became nine, and a young fellow name of Norman Rha took the art to the United States.

Now, not to sidestep, but before we continue with Norman Rha and the Kang Duk Won, we have to re-approach this story from another angle.

There was a Korean, Choi Yeong-eui, who was born in 1923. This Korean wanted to study Karate, and eventually he would go to Japan.

In Japan he was considered a very lowly person. He was picked on, bullied, beaten, and, in one tale, thrown to the ground and pissed on.

All of which did nothing more than, sorry about the pun, piss young Choi off.

He went into the mountains and dedicated himself to learning Karate.

He set up a grueling training regimen, which included work outs in the snow and breaking boulders with his bare hands.

And, after a year, he decided he wasn't done, so he stayed in the mountains for another year.

And, he returned to civilization, beat the hell out of all who had suppressed him, and became famous for killing bulls with his bare hands.

His Japanese name was...Mas Oyama.

Mas spent time in the United States, and his favorite American was a fellow name of Don Buck.

Mr. Buck was known as the tiger of Benecia, and he was one of the first people to open a karate school in the United States.

And, a short aside, Don was a weight lifter, boxer, wrestler, physical cultist, and a a police officer. One day he was bashed on the head by a bad guy, and was retired from the police department. From a life threatening injury, one that would rattle the brains of a normal person, Mr. Buck rehabilitated himself through the martial arts, and became a definite influence on the martial arts in America.

One of the first people to walk through Mr. Buck's doors was a young fellow name of Bob Babich.

Bob studied hard, and became one of Mr. Buck's first black belts, and one of his first instructors.

And, one day, who should walk into the studio but a young Korean, fresh off the boat, couldn't speak much English, but...Norman Rha.

Norman, though slight and short, fit right in with the fanatical Mr. Buck. He was polite, freestyled like a maniac, and knew Karate.

But, the karate he knew was different.

Don Buck was trained in the muscular, stand there and take a punch in the face and keep training school.

Norman was trained in the Kang Duk Won. Move quick, move fast, don't get hit.

And, an aside, apparently Yoon had slanted his karate, and influenced it with his Chuan Fa, which included what this writer calls 'The Tong Bei influence.'

Tong Bei is an internal system, apparently based on internal principles much like Tai chi or Hsing I. The Kang Duk Won, as you will come to understand when we enter the section on matrixing, has low stances and has a certain catlike fluidity to its moves.

The point is that we have two karate systems with the same forms...that are totally different.

Mr. Buck, realizing that the two systems wouldn't work well together, told Bob Babich to go with Norman.

So Bob lived with Norman, perhaps teaching Norman the English language in return for the Kang Duk Won.

Bob reached the rank of 6th black belt, and brought the Kang Duk Won to its highest level.

And, this author had the blessing to be able to study with Bob Babich.

Thus, though not many people know of these histories, they provide a nexus for some amazing martial arts.

People who don't get promoted, organizations that become rogue, politics, entrepreneurship. Internal martial arts with external arts, chuan fa 'leaving the fold,' then coming back together.

It is a most interesting history.

And, it provided a platform for the author to discover Matrixing.

What's Wrong with Kenpo (part one)

In asking this question, 'What's Wrong with Kenpo,' the author realizes he has already created ill will.

And he hopes to distill that ill will through the science of matrixing.

If people can actually look at what is happening, what happened, and see where Kenpo goes awry, then perhaps they will be willing to put it straight, and to elevate Kenpo.

But, first one has to be willing to admit that there could be something wrong with it.

So, my apologies, but here we go...

All martial arts are messed up. They are tweaked to fit tournaments, or designed solely for war, or altered for commercial purposes (to make money), and so on.

With Kenpo, however, we can look at several specific items that have contributed to the mess. This has actually been the purpose of the short history I have provided you with.

The fact of the matter is that:

James Mitose claims to have learned Kenpo from priests in a buddhist temple. Yet, there are possibilities that this isn't so.

Mitose taught the art for self-defense during world war two, which may have included alterations for the times and people.

While Mitose conducted himself with honor, the people around him were not always so inclined, and this may have had effect.

Thunderbolt Chow might have had lineage to Buddhist temples, but there is the distinct possibility that he didn't.

He made no secret about preferring, and thus slanting, his teachings to street techniques.

Ed Parker: his rank is in doubt, he changed his system five times, he might have been dishonest with the (alleged?) co-author of one his books.

The Tracy Brothers: might have been true to the source of Kenpo, but is that good? Considering that there might be questions about the legitimacy of those earlier arts?

Adding such novelties as contracts, which, true or not, many people hold as the death of the martial arts.

Rod Martin's ranking is in doubt.

The above stated, we are not interested in the good nor the bad of those earlier pioneers and geniuses, for they strived, they made mistakes, but those mistakes were based on what they had, what they were presented with, and the fact is that these things have been going on in the martial arts since time immemorial.

So let's look at the science of Matrixing, and then return to the technical side of what is wrong with Kenpo.

Matrixing

Matrixing is a science. It is proof in itself from a simple viewpoint: the body is a machine; it is a motor, and acts like a motor, and can be utilized using 'motorific' principles.

A motor, to function, needs to be bolted down.

A car engine is 'bolted' to the frame through the use of motor mounts. Without these struts to keep it in place the motor would turn over and flop on the ground. Bolted in place, it is able to transmit energy into the vehicle to be utilized for propulsion and other things.

A motor needs to be properly aligned, and a body, likewise, needs to be properly aligned lest it collapse under the impact and stress of weight.

A motor needs fuel. In fact, it needs multiple substances to function. This includes oil, gas, hydraulic fluid, air, and so on. In a body this includes oxygen, water, and food stuffs.

So let's look at how the 'motor' of the body is actually used in the martial arts.

There are four 'basic/basics' in the martial arts. Interestingly, if you look at classic writings on the subject, you will find these basic/basics lightly, and not always correctly, described. These basic/basics are crucial to the martial arts, and must be used in ALL basics, ALL motions, ALL aspects of the martial arts.

The four basic/basics are:

relaxing

breathing

grounding

alignment

There can be other basic/basics, but these will be specific to an art. The basic/basics I have listed are common to ALL martial arts.

If you have them, as I describe them, then your art is true. If you don't, then your is not.

Or perhaps I should state this differently.

To the degree that you have basic/basics, to that degree is your art true. And to the degree that you do not have basic/basics, to that degree your art is not true.

Relaxing means that you are not running energy through your body, and specifically in a manner that opposes your body.

Breathing is essential to the coordination of motion, or what I call Coordinated Body Motion (CBM), which I will describe in a few paragraphs. The rules of breathing are simple. Breath out when the body expands, breath in when it contracts. Breath out when you strike or are getting struck. And that is actually it. That's the whole thing, yet you would be shocked at how many people abuse this simple rule.

Grounding is when you sink the weight. This connects the motor to the ground and enables it to function properly and with authority.

Alignment is when somebody pushes on the body and the stress travels through the body and into the ground. Every technique, every motion of every technique, should be tested for this.

Now, if you have these basic/basics working in all of your basics, then you have a solid and true martial art.

Unfortunately, in the case of Kenpo, there is too much motion to solidly nail down these basics. The hands are moving too fast, and one can't always coordinate the breathing, or the grounding, or the alignment.

This is a massive error, and the only way to correct it is to simplify some of the basics, to take them apart and make sure you snap the hips at the right time to create alignment, change stances more, and sink the weight with all the changes and alignments, and so on.

In the section on techniques I will often say that a technique is too busy. This can refer to several things, but especially the fact that things are moving so fast the basic/basics aren't being properly utilized.

At this point, before moving on, let's consider a fifth basic/basic. This is the 'loose-tight' aspect of a strike or block; relaxing and then focusing the energy into one moment.

This particular basic/basic is specific to Karate, and it can be included in some techniques in Kenpo.

However, the loose-tight concept is often neglected because of the circularity and speed of the hands. Thus, the concept should be altered to some sort of loose, circular through many motions, to a tight in the strike.

This is the way one would handle it in Kenpo. However, every art has its own specific extra basic/basic, or concept upon which the art is based. Sometimes the concept works, and the basic/basic can be nailed down. Harmony is Aikido comes to mind, or absorbing the strike in Tai Chi Chuan.

So, whether you are doing Kenpo, or a concept in kenpo that is actually from another art, or another art entirely, one must become aware of the existence of an extra basic/basic, and one must learn how to do that concept effectively, efficiently, and at the right time.

We now come to a concept called CBM, or Coordinated Body Motion. I mentioned this concept a bit earlier in this book.

CBM is when all parts of the body begin motion at the same time, and end motion at the same time. And, all parts of the body must be adjusted so that they draw the correct and appropriate amount of energy according to the mass and motion of the body part.

And, this concept is also neglected in Kenpo. Also, the idea of being too busy in your motion can hurt the implementation of CBM.

Now, one last concept to go into before we start analyzing kenpo specifically.

CBM is not just when the body parts align in motion, it is when you coordinate sinking the weight, proper body alignment, breathing, and ALL the parts of the body.

CBMing the thrust of the body, the turn of the hips, and the sinking of the weight, create power. In fact, doing these three things in a CBM fashion will actually cause your body to manufacture Ki, or chi.

Okay, there is a lot more to matrixing than just these concepts, but these are enough to get you started in matrixing Kenpo. For a more in depth analysis of Matrixing I recommend the Matrixing Karate Series. Right now, let's take a more in depth look at what is wrong with Kenpo.

What's Wrong with Kenpo (part two)

Following are eleven things that are wrong with Kenpo. I am going to be mentioning these things as we analyze the individual techniques, but for right now, let's take a look at each item. There is no particular order to this evaluation of Kenpo.

One, there is the problem of translating Karate into Kenpo. Karate is more linear, and it is the first art that Parker studied, and it was core to the art taught by Mitose, and most likely that of Chow. It is likely that Kung Fu came in with Jimmy Woo. The problem here is that it is difficult to mount circularity on a karate stance. It just doesn't seem to translate easily, and the result is that the power of karate becomes corrupted, and the flow of the hands becomes subdued. Kenpo has worked around some of these problems, but you should know that the problems are still there, even if only hiding in the evolution of certain techniques and motions.

Two, there is the problem of posing. Posing is when the attacker has to hold his position while the defender works the technique. This causes a high degree of unreality, and builds a fantasy in the defender's mind, or at least an unreal expectation of what is happening in reality.

Three, there is a severe unreality inherent in training exclusively in air techniques. One NEEDS an opponent. One must not slash the air and think he is deadly, for he never learns about impact and the weight of bodies and the realities of a real fight.

Four, the techniques are random and out of order. This refuses logic, and makes the method harder to learn. Consider it this way: if something is easy to learn and easy to remember, it will be easy to use. It is simply a matter of introducing logic to the method. Logic, of course, is what matrixing is all about.

Five, there are better ways of teaching. Currently, the teaching is done mostly one on one, and this is done because it fits with the car contract method of signing people up. It would be far better to, for one instance, group people in small groups of four, have them work on specific things, for instance, escapes. Then, after a few months, one is ready for the next group of techniques. This may become more apparent as we go through the individual techniques. For now, let me just recommend the following sequence: go from escapes to single punches to weapons takedowns to multiple strikes. This is only one of many ways to restructure Kenpo.

Sixth, the forms are a mess. They are nothing more than doing the techniques in sequence. There is no logic, or isolation of principle, or anything else. There are far better ways of doing forms, and after we have gone through the techniques I will give you advice on how to restructure forms so that they are logical, easy to do, and actually go someplace.

Seventh, doing the techniques on one side only. One should ALWAYS learn how to do the techniques on both sides, and at the same time. To not do so is to actually unbalance the body.

Eight, there are two arts, the art of kenpo, and the art of freestyle. There must be some resolution to this factor for the art to be truly effective.

Nine, there are two arts, the art of escaping, which is more like a rarified jujitsu (which doesn't always work, or is complex instead of simple), and the hand techniques for defending against strikes.

Ten, some of the techniques shift the distance in an unworkable way. Moves should progress from kick to punch to knee to elbow to takedown. Yes, there are going to be exceptions, but this is a general rules that is constantly broken in Kenpo.

Eleven, the hand strikes are presented in a strange mix, which will be described in the 'Matrix of Motion in Kenpo' in the section following this one. This mix presents techniques in a sometimes unworkable way.

There are more things wrong, but I have done enough damage for right now; you have a LOT to think about. But, at least you will know what I am talking about now when we begin analyzing the individual techniques.

Matrixing Motion in Kenpo

A matrix is a graph that illuminates certain factors. For a fuller description of matrix graphs, including how to make them, I recommend the Matrixing Karate series, and other writings I have done on matrixing.

For now, I want to write one matrix. This is not going to be a graph so much as a list. Lists, just so you know were my earliest efforts at matrixing. I simply wrote down everything I could so that I could understand all the potentials involved. This particular list, or matrix, I call the matrix of motion in Kenpo.

In Kenpo there are only so many things you can do, and still remain true to the concept of Kenpo. Here are the Kenpo arm motions.

block and counter on same side

block and counter on opposite side

block and rolling counter on same side

block and rolling counter on opposite side

And, there are ways of mixing these concepts, and these ways don't always work.

But...Kenpo techniques usually fall into one of these categories, or a mix of these categories.

The block and counter usually refers to a karate style defense. It will have limbs going back and forth and not with any degree of circularity.

Same side means you are doing everything with one hand. For instance, an outward block and a strike, both with the right hand.

Opposite side refers to block with one hand, and strike with the other. There will be more balance with this type of move. in fact, opposite side is more basic, and same side is going to be more advanced.

Block and rolling counter refers to the fact that the arm is not starting and stopping, starting and stopping, thus moving in opposing directions within the same technique, but rather starting once and then rolling through motion to a final and single stop. This is more of a kung fu-ish movement.

Same side and opposite side are as described for this rolling, kung fu movement as they are in the harder karate style movement.

And, I include the snapping movements, which seem to almost bounce off once self or an opponent in the rolling category. This because you are using something to keep the motion going, and not just using your own set of muscles to start the motion and stop the motion, start the motion and stop the motion.

Now, if you load too many motions on one side then that side becomes 'too busy.' This leads to unreal techniques, poser techniques, and so on.

Conclusion to the History

Okay, you can see where I am going with this.

You can see that I am scientifically analyzing the amount of motion, and the type of motion, in order to categorize kenpo techniques according to error.

And, hopefully, to label a technique as workable and logical, a fit technique for inclusion in a corrected form of Kenpo which we will call 'Matrix Kenpo,' or at least to offer corrections so that we can, again, include the technique in a better and more improved version of Kenpo.

Now, it is time to go through the techniques.

After we go through the techniques we will look at the final results and recompile kenpo, this in a more scientific manner.

We will also discuss further potential matrixes so that you can find hidden techniques, better illuminate mistakes and avenues of thought.

And we will come up with a better method for doing the forms. Forms, I should add, that are based on corrected Kenpo techniques.

35

Part Two
Kenpo Techniques

A List of Kenpo Techniques

Following is the list of techniques that I learned in Kenpo under Rod Martin. Many of these techniques you will recognize from other variations of Kenpo. Sometimes you will note differences in names, sometimes whole transformations of techniques. Sometimes you may not recognize anything. That's okay, I went through the lineage earlier, and while the various instructors obviously changed the art to suit themselves, there should be sufficient truth in this list to qualify it as a good representation of Kenpo.

And, there will be mistakes in this list, mistakes I have made, either in the original notes, or in the reading of these notes over forty years later.

Techniques for Orange Belt

1. Flapping Wing ~ two hand label
2. Twisted Wing ~ Armlock
3. Escape of the Lamb ~ two hand choke from rear
4. Evading the Samurai ~ right punch
5. striking key ~ hand on shoulder from side
6. charging bull a ~ charge from front
7. entering the shrine a ~ bear hug from front arms loose
8. entering the shrine b ~ bear hug from front arms loose
9. entering the shrine c ~ bear hug from front arms loose
10. entering the shrine d ~bear hug from front arms loose
11. jaws of the tiger a ~ wrist grab same side
12. jaws of the tiger b ~ wrist grab same side
13. grasping honor a ~ shaking hands
14. grasping honor b ~ shaking hands
15. lobster claws a ~ holding wrists in front of body
16. sharpening the blade a ~ lapel grab one hand
17. striking mallet ~ two hands grab wrist in front of body
18. flower of buddha ~ standing from Indian sitting
19. chopping bamboo a ~ two man shoulder grab from sides
20. charging bull b ~ charge from front
21. charging bull c ~ charge from front
22. wounded paws ~ bear hug from rear arms loose
23. capturing paws a ~ bear hug from rear arms trapped
24. twisting the jaws ~ wrist grab cross side
25. tangled wings ~ full nelson
26. arrows from the sky ~ two handed lapel grab
27. coil of the python a ~ forearm around throat from rear
28. coil of the python b ~ forearm around throat from the rear
29. hidden sword a ~ two handed lapel grab
30. hidden sword b ~ two hand lapel pull
31. hand of the dragon ~ one hand to throat
32. doors of the shrine ~ front bear hug arms pinned
33. front bear hug arms pinned
34. releasing the vice a ~ headlock
35. releasing the vice b ~ headlock

36. releasing the vice c ~ headlock
37. descending arrow a ~ two hand choke from rear
38. descending arrow b ~ two hand choke from rear
39. sharpening the blade b ~ lapel grab with one hand
40. capturing paws b ~ bear hug from rear with arms pinned
41. tangled wings b ~ full nelson
42. chopping bamboo b ~ two man shoulder grabs from sides

Techniques for Purple Belt

1. Ram's head ~ overhead (club) attack
2. Cocking the Bow ~ overhead (club) attack
3. Sacred Chopsticks ~ kick
4. Eagle's Grasp ~ shoulder grab from side
5. Charging Bull D ~ charge from front
6. Charging Bull E ~ charge from front
7. Crouching Cat ~ punch from side
8. Chinese Servant ~ punch from side
9. Twisted Wing B ~ armlock
10. Twisted Wing C ~ armlock
11. Broken Hourglass ~ shoulder grab cross side
12. Sacred Spike ~ knee attack
13. Flashing Thong ~ two punches
14. Broken Honor A ~ shaking hands
15. Descending Arrow C ~ two hand choke from rear
16. Descending Arrow D ~ two hand choke from rear
17. Descending Arrow E ~ two hand choke from rear
18. Twisted Wing D ~ armlock
19. Twisted Wing E ~ armlock
20. Hidden Key A ~ two hand lapel grab
21. Lifting the Chopsticks A ~ overhead (club) attack
22. Key to the Sword ~ shoulder grab from side
23. Snapping the Limb ~ punch
24. Sting of the Bee ~ punch
25. Ox Cart ~ two hand choke from rear
26. Flapping Wing C ~ two hand lapel grab

27. Flapping Wing D ~ two hand lapel grab
28. The Shield ~ punch
29. Sacred Sacrifice ~ kick when kneeling
30. Descending Arrow E ~ two hand choke from rear
31. Lifting the Chopsticks B ~ overhead (club) attack
32. Fluttering Leaves ~ two hand grab to throat from front
33. Slaying the Dragon ~ punch
34. Burning Cinders ~ two hand to throat (or lapel) from front
35. Lightening Flash A ~ knife thrust to belly
36. Lightening Flash B ~ knife thrust to belly
37. Lightening Flash C ~ knife thrust to belly
38. Hidden Key B ~ two handed lapel grab
39. Flapping Wing E ~ two handed lapel grab
40. Clinging Vines ~ two man grabbing wrists from each side

Techniques for Blue Belt

1. Thousand Mallets ~ punch
2. Parting the Beads ~ two hand push to chest
3. Releasing the Eagle ~ shoulder grab same side
4. Tumbling Samurai ~ push from behind
5. Escape of the Lamb B ~ two hand choke from rear
6. Lobster's Claws B ~ two hand wrists grabbed from front
7. Chinese eclipse ~ punch
8. Lobster's Claws c ~ two hands grabbing wrists from front
9. Crumbling Statue A ~ punch
10. Whirlpool ~ right punch
11. Silkscreen A ~ left shoulder grab with right punch
12. Ox Cart B ~ two hand choke from rear
13. Hand of the Dragon B ~ one hand on throat
14. Hand of the Dragon C ~ one hand on throat
15. Hand of the Dragon D ~ one hand on throat
16. Driving the Spike ~ punch
17. Crossing Swords ~ punch
18. Tangled Wings C ~ defense for full nelson
19. Siege of the Temple ~ two man attack, front and rear

20. Broken Honor B ~ defense for a handshake
21. Hoofs of Death ~ punch
22. Spinning Blades ~ punch from side
23. Crossed Arrows ~ two man attack, front and rear
24. Wings of Iron A ~ punch
25. Wings of Iron B ~ punch
26. Crashing Waves ~ two hands to the throat
27. Clawing Hawk ~ two hands to the throat
28. Spreading Wings A ~ two man attack from sides
29. Spreading Wings B ~ two man attack from sides
30. Silk Screen B/C ~ grab and punch
31. Striking Cobra A ~ two punches
32. Striking Cobra B ~ two punches
33. Striking Cobra C ~ two punches
34. Blinding Sword ~ punch
35. Revealing Vest ~ bear hug
36. Sealing the Chest ~ punch
37. Sculpturing Buddha ~ two hand choke from front

Techniques for Green Belt

1. Circling Fans ~ punch from side
2. Shield of Death ~ punch
3. Dancing Cat ~ two punch combination
4. Slashing Claws ~ two punches
5. Snapping the Vines ~ two man grab from sides
6. Fallen Warrior A ~ shoulder grab
7. Rickshaw ~ grab and knee in back
8. Flapping Wing D ~ lapel grab
9. Striking the Gong ~ right punch
10. Wielding the Torch ~ two punches
11. Soaring Eagle ~ punch
12. Glancing Blades ~ punch
13. Thundering Clouds ~ shoulder grab from side
14. Jewels of Blackness ~ punch
15. Flight of the Swan ~ punch

16. Ox Cart C ~ two handed choke from rear
17. Rising Sun ~ right punch back to wall
18. Fallen Warrior B ~ grab to shoulder
19. Breaking the Yoke A ~ two handed choke from rear
20. Gun Attack A ~ gun
21. Flaming Dragon ~ punch from side
22. Lifting the Chopsticks C ~ overhead club attack
23. Breaking the Yoke B ~ two handed choke from rear
24. Slaying the Dragon B ~ punch
25. Slamming Gate A ~ roundhouse punch
26. Shifting Sails ~ punch
27. Jaws of the Tiger C ~ wrist grab
28. Jaws of the Tiger D ~ wrist grab
29. Jaws of the Tiger E ~ wrist grab
30. Jaws of the Tiger F ~ wrist grab
31. Glancing Tong ~ punch
32. Shifting Current A ~ punch
33. Crumbling Statue B ~ punch
34. Gun Attack B ~ gun
35. Key to Darkness ~ punch
36. Shifting Current B ~ punch
37. Shifting Current C ~ punch combination
38. Slamming Gate B ~ roundhouse club attack
39. Jaws of the Tiger G ~ wrist grab
40. Siamese Cat ~ punch

Techniques for Brown Belt

1. Eagle Claw
2. Eagle Miss
3. Brown Club Attack
4. Brown Side Punch #4
5. Brown Side Punch #5
6. Brown Kick-Punch
7. Right-left/Left-right
8. Crossed Swords B

Orange Belt Techniques

Chapter One
Flapping Wing

Escape from two handed grasp on lapels.
But what if the attacker has bent elbows?

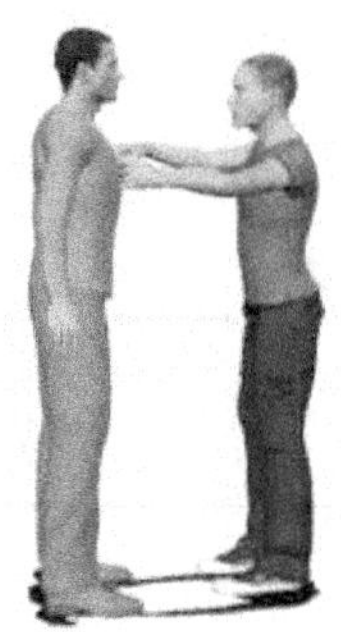 

Lock attacker's hands with left hand, as you step back with the left leg into a horse stance, and bring the right forearm up and break the elbows.

This twists your body so it is not aligned. There is no body, line of energy, or any other source of power for the upward breaking forearm.

Bring the right forearm around and down on the radial nerves.
Takes years to find and be able to savage the radials.
When doing the technique by yourself bounce the fist off the belly.
Yes. Good timing technique.
Chop the throat with the right hand.
Yes!

EXITING A TECHNIQUE

Pivot to kneeling position as you do a vertical hammer fist to the groin. Rear kick to the body and cross out to ready position.

Classic Kenpo method for exiting a technique. If you have done the technique and made it work, you shouldn't be running. You should be shoving the attacker into other attackers.

There is also a lot of motion here. The real technique stopped with the chop to the throat.

That said, I have nothing against exiting a technique as a matter of form. I mean, what's the alternative, stand there? Heck, get out of the way and let the dummy fall!

Chapter Two
Twisted Wing

Escape from an armlock. (left arm locked)

This is assuming a particular type of grasp by the attacker, but's not a bad technique.

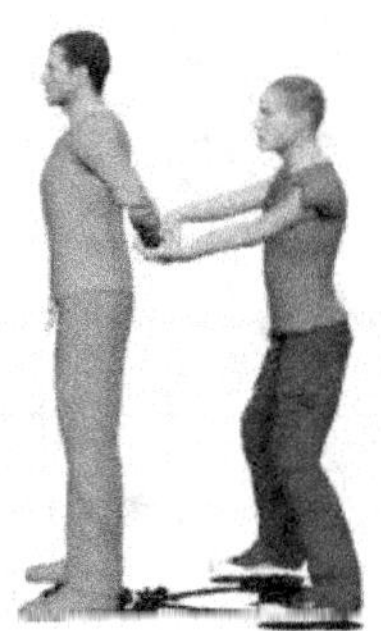 

Step back with right leg into horse stance as you execute a right elbow spike to the face.

Grasp Attacker's holding arm with your left hand as you step forward with the right leg into a horse stance, turning to face to the rear.

This is a complete 360 turn. A little unwieldy, even after an elbow to face.

Pulling the attacker's arm straight with your left hand, execute an armbar.

Right snap kick to belly, set forward in a horse while pulling the arm straight.

You actually end up a little jammed for space, too close for a kick. You can switch feet (Pop kick).

Also, pulling with the left hand and kicking with the right foot, in this closed space tends to mess with the alignment of the body if you aren't careful.

Break elbow with right elbow strike.

Nothing wrong with breaking an elbow. I think it would be a bit better to teach a takedown at this point. But there is a lot of room for opinion here.

Chapter Three
Escape of the Lamb

Escape from two handed choke from rear.

The problem here is that people don't usually choke with two straight arms.

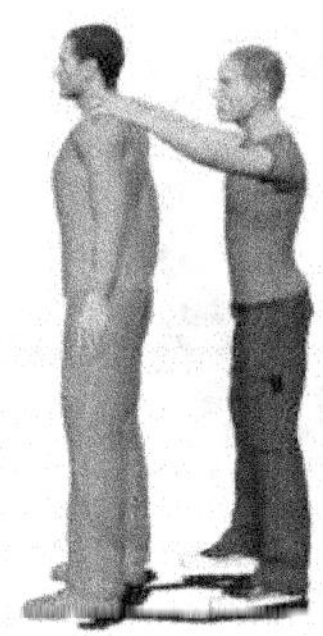 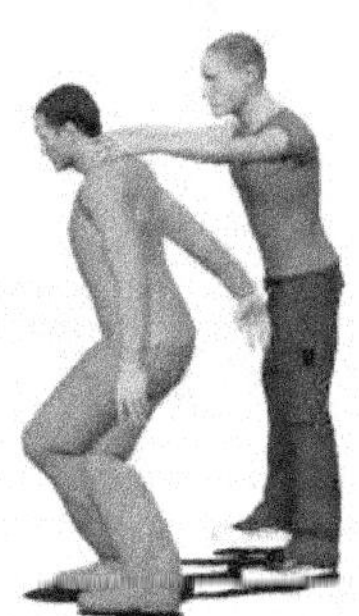

Bend forward and step behind the right leg with the left leg as you chop to the groin.

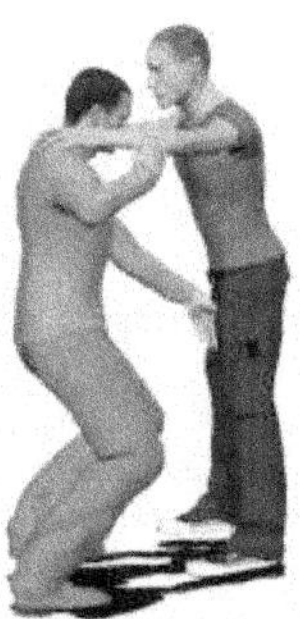

Pivot under the grip and execute a ridge hand to the groin.

Cross step with the left foot and step out to set.

The first thing wrong you can spot without matrixing. It is a basic basketball principle that one should not cross the legs when running a screen. This technique proves that. A simple push when stepping and you will be sent ass over teakettle.

The key to this technique lies in the simple advise that you should be breaking his wrist when you twist.

This is true. But it takes a weird degree of knowledge to break a wrist with a neck twist. Can be done. But...

That said, if you grab the hands so they can't let go and then do the technique...then you can brea the wrists. Cool.

EXCEPT, you are spinning, <u>while ducking, into a potential knee</u>.

So why not just set out in a horse and strike the groin? Take out the cross step (unless you are doing a grab art to break the wrists), and just go into a horse, then follow up with other techniques.

All too often you confuse arts here. This is unworkable kung fu with a cross step, but with a workable karate chop to the groin.

Chapter Four
Evading the Samurai

Blocking a Right Punch.

Great technique. Good for a beginner, will morph into faster more compact techniques with dedicated practice. Yes, we could use a grabbing block on the attacker's right hand, but that will develop naturally, or with very light instruction.

Step to the left with the left foot as you execute a right outward block.

Wheel kick to the mid-section.
Ready in the cat stance.

Chapter Five
Striking Key

Escape from hand on shoulder. Side by side, left hand on right shoulder. Attacker about to punch.

This isn't bad, just predicated on the idea of being able to strike the ulnar nerve. Takes a while to hit those nerves, probably not a good idea for a beginning. A beginner should be learning to break things, not pressure point them.

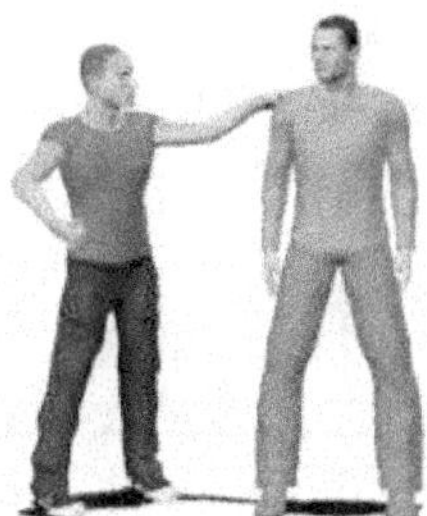

Reach across and lock the left hand in place with your left hand.

Strike up into the ulnar nerve with the middle knuckle of your right hand.
Strike armpit with same hand.

Knife Edge Side Kick to the knee.

Here's the real problem. The knife kick is one of those kicks that will break your foot. Go ahead, walk on a knife edge. You won't last long, and you expect to hit with authority?

What probably happened is that the original guys, a hundred years ago, were slapping the knee with the outside of their foot, like a lower level crescent kick. that would work, and it might even fit in with the clothes of the time.

One alternative would be to stomp the knee with a straight side thrust kick. Problem with that is that it takes time to lift the knee, and you are now angling a kick into a joint. Makes for weird targeting.

The best alternative would be to maybe roll the elbow a bit with the palm, lurching the guy off balance, and using a wheel kick with the instep to mess up the leg and set up a takedown.

Chapter Six
Charging Bull

Avoiding rush (takedown) from the front.

I'm going to be critical here, but don't mistake me, I like this technique. It has some excellent points for handling a front rush, as one might encounter from a Mixed Martial Artist when trying for a single or double leg takedown.

Kick to the groin, set back in horse stance.

The problem is that the kick passes right through the hands. Makes it prone to being grabbed. There is also the assumption that the attacker will crumple over the kick. Maybe, more likely back when nobody knew martial arts, not as likely these days.

Chop to the back of the neck with the left hand.

This is what I like. I have seen it work, and work well, against attacker's trying for this takedown. The only reason you don't see it in modern MMA matches, I believe, is because I think it is illegal. And that brings up an interesting question: why would something be illegal unless it worked TOO well?

BUT, I would recommend an elbow smash to the head instead of the chop.

Chapter Seven
Entering the Shrine A

Escape from bear hug from the front, hugging arms inside your arms.

The problem is in the question...how many people do a bear hug without trying to trap the hands? Still, the assumption here is fine for teaching a beginner.

Grab hair and pull.

My poser guy has short hair, so grab into eyes, grab ears, grab something if you want to make this thing work. An interesting lesson: if you throw something small, like a pinkie, off a cliff, and there is some pain involved to shut down his analytical ability, his whole body will follow that pinkie.

Step forward and strike Adam's apple with half fist.

So what are his arms going to be doing while you're doing all this?

Chapter Eight
Entering the Shrine B

Escape from bear hug from the front, hugging arms inside your arms.

I like this one. If you sink your weight and use your stance properly, the fellow will be drawn off balance, and even though you are a little twisted, the back of the neck is a great target.

Step back and strike the back of the neck with the forearm.

Strike with the other forearm.
Strike with the forearm.

Chapter Nine
Entering the Shrine C

Escape from bear hug from the front, hugging arms inside your arms.

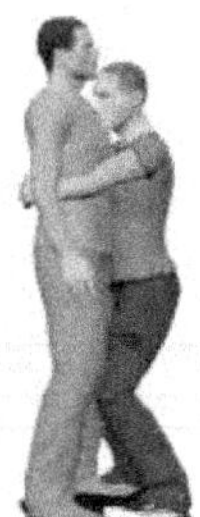 

Push the side of the head with one hand as you strike with the middle knuckle below the ear.

Another interesting technique. Would a strike really be good? The second hand bracing sounds like it should be a grind into the nerve center below the ear. This would work great, except that it takes a lot of practice to locate pressure points and nerve centers. That said, some of the other things you could do are grind the chin into an eye socket, bite, use your hands to claw parts of his face, and so on.

One thing you want to avoid is losing balance. If he's hugging, he's wrestling, and if wrestling is his strong point you want to avoid it.

Chapter Ten
Entering the Shrine D

Escape from bear hug from the front, hugging arms inside your arms.

Strike temples with heels of hands.

Palm heels to the temples? Temples are the thinnest bones in the skull, I believe, so why not just use fists? You want to break the bones, right?

Of course, maybe this was done to students, and you are expected to figure stuff out on your own.

That said, if you're hands are loose, I think this is probably the best, but there are so many other potentials here.

Stick your fingers in his eyes, lift his septum, stick a finger or two into his neck and just dig...

But that's the glory of Kenpo...lots of choices, lots of doors to go through.

As I said, figure out stuff on your own.

That's the purpose of these books, to examine the techniques, the physics, the stories, and to enable you to get creative in your thinking and find out what really works for you.

Chapter Eleven
Jaws of the Tiger A

Escape from right wrist grab to the left wrist.

Another good one, especially to build the basic understanding of how the body works. Breaking loose from the grip can be done better with some aiki studies (circling the joint), and the arm extended across the front of the body is not good, as it traps one's own hand. Still, the forward motion will usually slow the attacker's response.

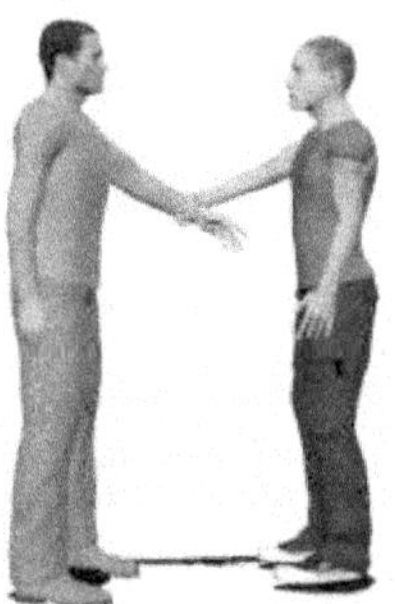
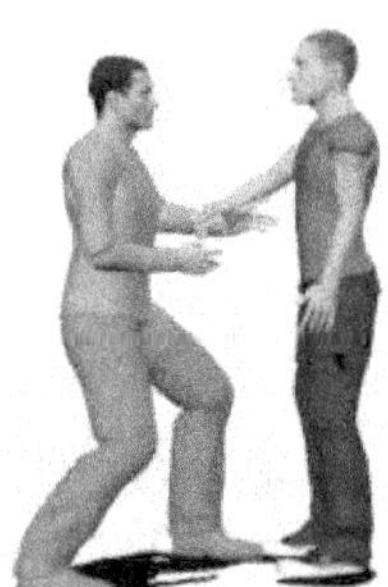

Step forward with the left leg and bring the left arm back

Extend across body, execute a right outward block.

A study of body alignment, as to squaring the hips, then aligning them with the curve of the body, would be good. One of the big weaknesses of kenpo is the missed opportunities to learn and use hips. The hips are the cornerstone of the whole body weight.

Left punch to ribs, then right punch to head.

Again, use the hips when punching, if only a little. You can increase the power of the punch by MUCH simply by turning the hips into the punches.

Chapter Twelve
Jaws of the Tiger B

Escape from right wrist grab to the left wrist.

Excellent technique, if you remember that you must lower the elbow, and the hips, before shooting your hand up.

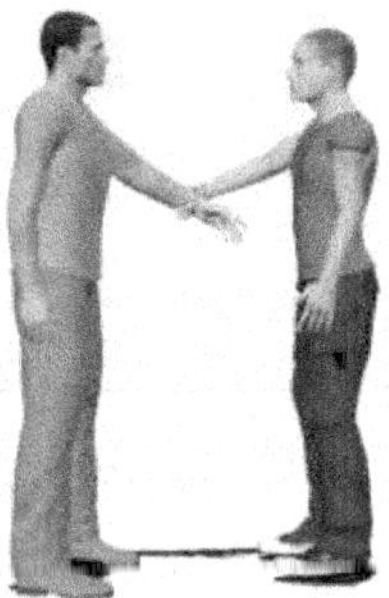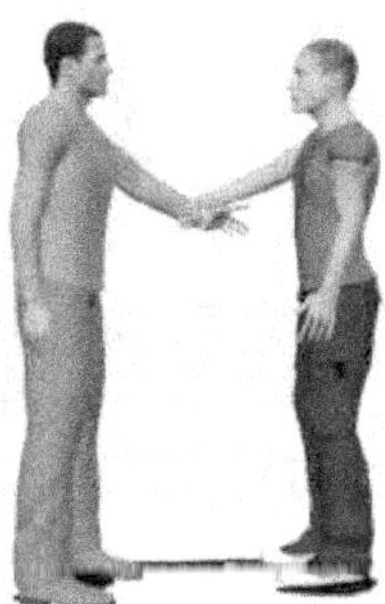

Form a Y with thumb and index of the left hand and lift his arm up.

Step forward with the left foot and execute a left downward elbow spike to the chest.

You should hold the hips somewhat square when raising the arm, then turn into a horse stance as you drop the elbow. This will provide hip twist and more effective grounding.

Consider shooting a palm to the face, instead of just thrusting upwards.

Chapter Thirteen
Grasping honor A

Attack while shaking hands.

Okay, great technique for a punch, or some other situation, but...shaking hands? So are you a creep to be making a show of friendliness and then cold cocking the guy with a knee?

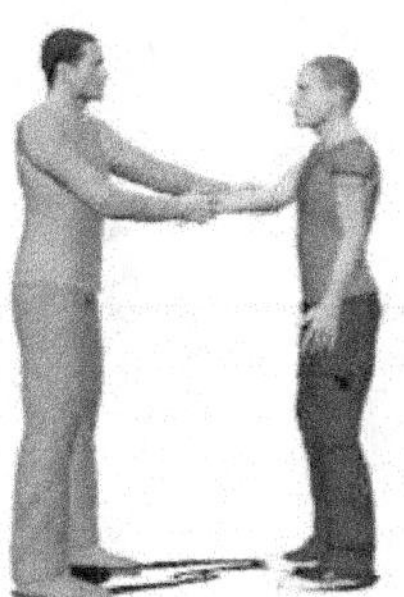

Grasp elbow with the left hand, step forward with the right leg as you pull.

Right horizontal knee to mid section.

I do have a slight problem with pulling the upper body to the right while hopping to the left with the lower body. This means the body is going in two directions, splits intention, robs power from the technique.

Well, maybe you didn't really want full power, and didn't really want to hurt him. I mean, he's shaking your hand!

Chapter Fourteen
Grasping Honor B

Attack while shaking hands.

Again, maiming somebody who wants to shake hands with you. Sheesh!

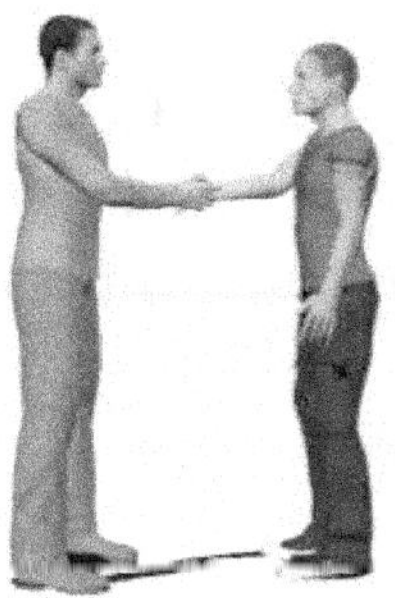 

Pull opponent to the right as you hop to the left.

Again, going one way with the upper body, and the other way with the lower body.

Side knife edge kick to knee.

Cross out and set.

Should use a straight side kick. I have noted before that kicking with the knife edge, unless you use it like a lower level crescent kick, will damage your own foot.

Add a punch after the handshake and this technique becomes real.

Chapter Fifteen
Lobster Claws

Attacker holding wrists down in front of body.

This is a good one, with a few quirks to mess it up.

First, dropping the weight is excellent. Good grounding, right out matrixing, and LOTS of other serious arts. One has to wonder about the direction of the step, however.

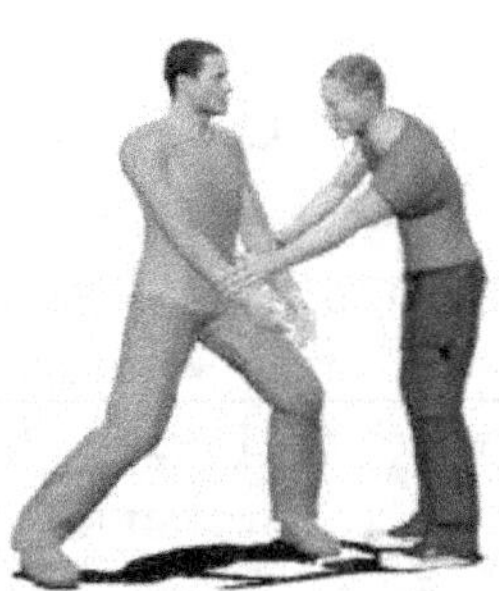

Step back to horse while pushing hands down.

Execute double outward blocks. Execute double low knife blocks to clear the hands.

Outward blocks are okay, but a simple headbutt, or a punch, or maybe a good solid elbow, would be more direct. There is just too much hand motion going on to expect the attacker not to be doing something in the mean time.

Snap kick to the groin.

I know beginners should use the rear foot to kick, but it is too slow when you are at hand distance. Best to learn how to kick with the front foot.

The real problem, however, is that defender is in the wrong stance for a kick with the front foot. Needs to be in a back stance.

Double palm strike to chest.

Palms don't hurt enough. Middle knuckles to the floating ribs would break them easily. (I know, I broke a student's once. Man, was I embarrassed!)

Floating ribs are great targets because they don't connect in the front, and if you angle the strike upwards they tend to snap. They bend in if you punch in, but they aren't constructed to bend if you strike up on them.

Chapter Sixteen
Sharpening the Blade

Defense against lapel grab with right hand.
Not a bad technique, up to a point.

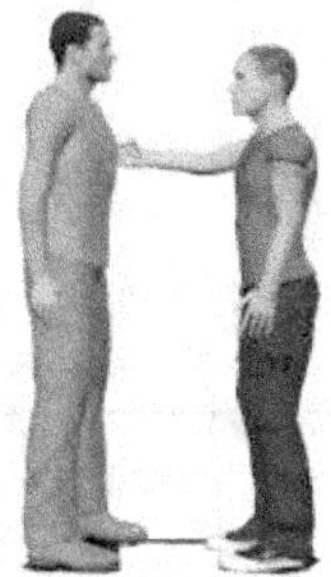 

Lock grab with the right hand.

Step back with the right foot into a horse stance as you break the elbow with a left inward block.

Rake down with the left forearm on the radial nerves.

Okay, you just broke an elbow. A lot of practice, this can work. Even if it doesn't, it's good for set ups and such. BUT, why would you want to paralyze an arm that is broken? Are we just practicing set ups? By itself, a downward rake is fine, sets up the throat chop. But it just doesn't fit with the motion of the break. One or the other, but not both.

Chop to the neck.
Cross out and set.

Chapter Seventeen
Striking Mallet

Two hands grasp wrist defense. Left wrist is grabbed.

Kick is great, but the escape from the grab has missed the boat. If you drop the elbow then you can shoot the hand, break thumbs and things, and punch the face (or whatever else).

I understand that you are giving a beginner, or a weak person, confidence in being able to break a grab, but the education is not to double up on the muscle, but to figure out the angles so that you use superior body parts, alignment, and leverage.

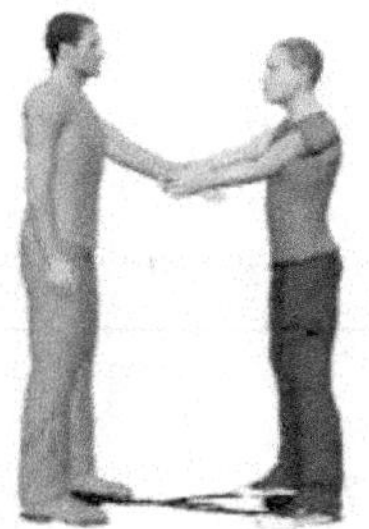 

Left front kick to groin.

Set down forward and grab left fist with the right hand.

Pull wrist up, breaking grab, and upward to execute a vertical elbow strike to the chin.

Pivot into a bow stance (front stance facing away).

Rear kick.

Cross over and set.

I'm a little surprised that the pivot only goes to a front stance. Normally, the classic kenpo move seems to be to a kneeling stance with a hammer to the groin. Just changing things up a bit, I guess.

Chapter Eighteen
Flower of Buddha

Attacked while sitting in a cross-legged position.

Rise and set.

Add secondary techniques as you wish.

I always liked this one. A simple exercise that strengthened the legs. A bit yogic, if you get my drift. We used to do a snap kick out of it, I believe. These days, courtesy of Matrixing, I would recommend doing Flower of Buddha and then plug in each and every technique. Don't do everything in one night. Take your time and practice two or three techniques every night. Make sure your legs can take the wear and tear before you jack it up.

Chapter Nineteen
Chopping Bamboo

Two Men Grab Shoulders from each side.

One assumes certain things concerning this footwork. The first fellow is fine, but the second fellow is going to have to fall forward, which might happen, he might get pulled into the technique by not letting go when the defender starts moving.

Step forward slightly with the right leg while chopping to the side with the left hand.

Step forward with the left leg and pivot into horse while chopping with the left hand.

Cross step out and set.

The real problem is excessive time taken, because the second attacker is going to be doing something while you're stepping and turning..

Further, and maybe even more important, is that the stance is twisted, making transmission of power from the ground unlikely.

Chapter Twenty
Charging Bull B

Defense for a frontal rush.

A nice technique. Easy to do and makes sense. There is potential for grab arts here, but that can be explored later, when the beginner is more advanced.

Step back with the right foot into a horse stance as you execute a left elbow to the head and a right palm to the ear.

Cross out and set.

And, just a note, the horse stance fits the geometry of the arc of the elbow. The palm to the ear is a stretch, but acceptable. Well done.

Chapter Twenty-One
Charging Bull C

Defense for a frontal rush.

Another good one, one which makes sense and works, and especially as a defense against the MMA or jujitsu stylist, or even just a plain, old wrestler type, who opens with a single or double leg takedown. Especially adaptable once the rush has entered and the attacker is sufficiently bent over.

Step back into a horse stance as you execute an elbow spike to the center of the back and a hammerfist to the kidney.

Cross out and set.

Hammerfist isn't necessary, sort of superfluous. Again, might be better to look for a simple grab art of some sort.

Chapter Twenty-Two
Wounded Paws

Defense for bear hug from rear with arms free.

You know, it's not a bad idea to do these with the arms free at first. They aren't as realistic, but they are a gradient to arms trapped, allows the student a chance to learn. Unfortunately, the first time I ever had to make this work the fellow threw me on the floor. Yikes! See next chapter.

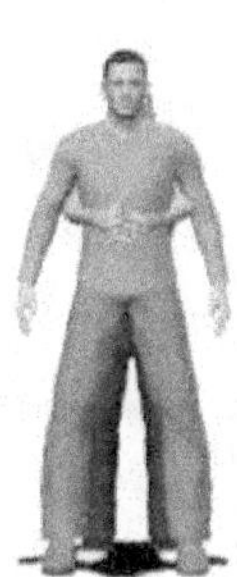

Circle arms out and up and then bring the elbows down on the attacker's hands as you sink into a horse stance.

Bring foot in, then step behind attacker into a horse stance, striking with an elbow to the neck to force over the horse.

You can see that my software went crazy trying to keep up with this one. And it drives home the first point, the guy won't hold you in a static position; he won't wait for you to do this technique.

And, as the image indicates, if you actually run this technique, and the doesn't let go of you, he is going to fall, and that means you'll now be supporting his weight, and that is going to put you off balance at best, and collapse you under him at worst.

Hammerfist to groin.

That all said, I still believe in this technique, but as the next chapter indicates, and as my collapsing software proves, there are some lessons to be learned here.

Chapter Twenty-Three
Capturing Paws

Defense for a bear hug from the rear with the arms trapped.

This is a very useful break. It is similar to the one I used in the last chapter. You can punch both arms to the front to set it up, and then the elbow works well, and there is nothing like a hammer to the groin to spice up the day of an attacker. I would add the fingers to the eyes with the left hand, which is right out of the Pinan Three form.

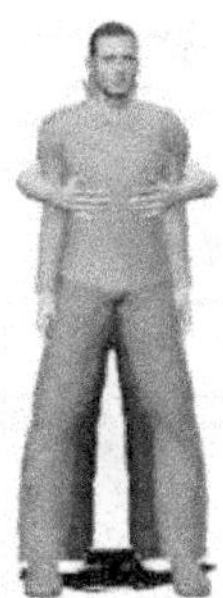

Step to the side into a horse as you execute an elbow strike.

Hammerfist to groin.

Chapter Twenty-Four
Twisting the Jaws

Attacker holds right wrist with right hand.

Interesting. This utilizes the whole body weight to pull the person into the technique. Excellent if you've a firm grip. The classical way to do this is to circle the wrist and step forward.

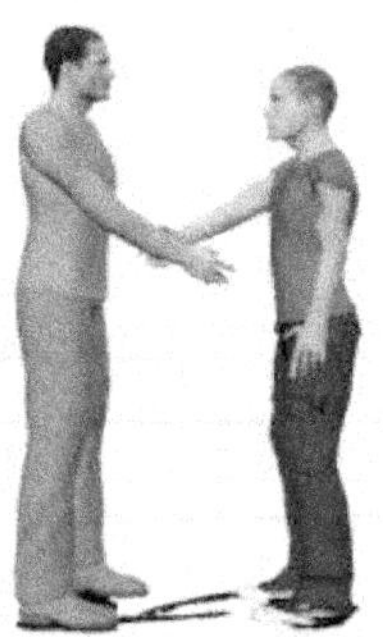

Circle the right wrist as you step back to a horse stance with the right foot.

Pull the arm straight break and execute a right elbow smash.

Right elbow to head.
Right elbow to back.
Hello Chiro!

Chapter Twenty-Five
Tangled Wings

Escape from a full nelson.

The problem with this technique is that you should handle it before anybody gets you in it. It takes some finagling to get somebody into a full nelson, so defeat before the lock is achieved.

Step to the left into a horse with the right leg as you strike temples with back knuckles.

From such an awkward position this strike would not have power, there is no body behind the backfist, which doesn't have any power anyway. At most, it is a distraction.

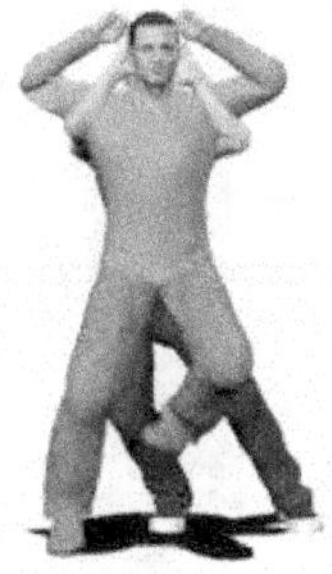

Left side knife edge kick to the inside of the left knee.
Left heel strike to the inside of the right knee.
Left side knife edge kick to the inside of the left knee.

Left stomp to instep.

The third kick to the inside of the knee, is it really necessary? Truth, the first one should have done the job, but I can understand, balance being at risk, having to do a couple.

As you can see, while there are things to be learned, because of the awkwardness of the strike and the threat to balance, I am not a big fan of this technique.

Even as a technique for beginners, it is sort of lame. Better to stick to the bread and butter and leave this for the tricky boys.

I don't recall, and my notes don't say, but there is possibly a cross out and set here. At least, it makes sense that there would be, this would introduce a turn as you leave an enemies territory.

Chapter Twenty-Six
Arrows from the Sky

Defense for a two handed lapel grab.

Time to make a defense is when the hands are on the way in, not when they have already achieved a grab. Also, the time spent moving the hands up and around is time that the attacker could be doing a lot of other things.

This technique definitely needs a quicker, faster, straight line application.

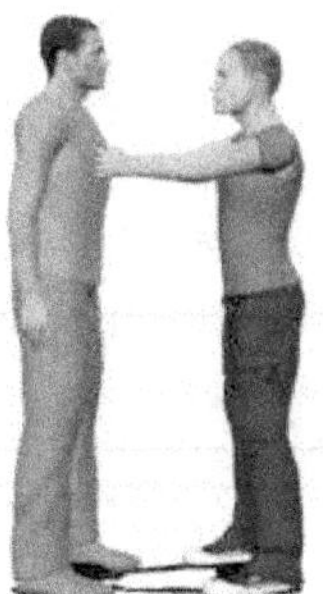

Step to the side as you bring the arms around, up and down on the forearms.

The above criticisms noted, the impact of the forearms on the wrists is excellent, as is the half fists to the throat. Though, one is enough. Using one hand allows the other hand to move in a way that will balance the sides of the body, or move into a protective mode, as is present in some other techniques.

Double half fist strikes to the throat.

Step forward with the right foot and execute an upward elbow strike to the chin.

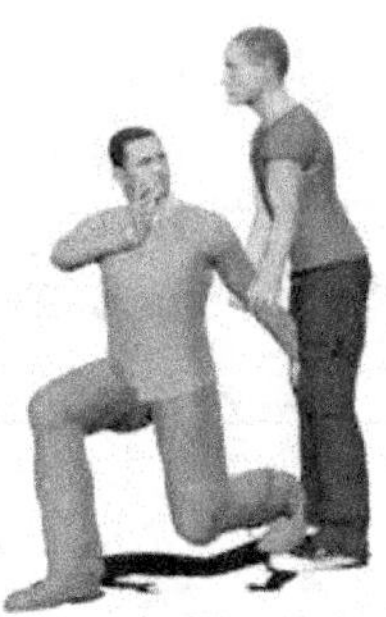

Pivot into a kneeling stance and do the cross out and set routine. (hammer groin, back kick to mid-section, step out and turn into set position.)

Chapter Twenty-Seven
Coil of the Python A

Forearm around throat from behind.

If somebody has got you around the neck, you should have moved when he was on the way in. If they have a forearm on your throat it is hard to sink the weight and pull that forearm with the throat. it takes more chi power than most people have, even many experienced martial artists.

Step to side as elbow to plexus.
Yes.

Hammerfist to groin.
Backfist to face.
Hammerfist is good, but backfist is weak. The hammerfist should probably be a groin grab.

The thing here is that you are standing there fighting while backwards. You should do something to bring him around to your front.

Chapter Twenty-Eight
Coil of the Python B

Forearm around throat from behind.

Grab choking arm and turn chin into the elbow.

A lot better! Grab the forearm to keep the pressure off, and push the neck into the elbow. He can't shorten his upper arm, so you have time.

Step into a horse and strike the solar plexus with the elbow.

Simultaneous hammerfist to groin and fingers to eyes.

Now the elbow will work. I would get rid of the hammerfist, maybe put the arm pull and neck turn into the last technique with the groin grab. Put the elbow to the plexus together with the eye jab.

Nice technique.

Chapter Twenty-Nine
Hidden Sword A

Defense for two handed lapel pull.

Excellent, little surprise. The attacker's sight of the ridgehand is obscured by his own arms.

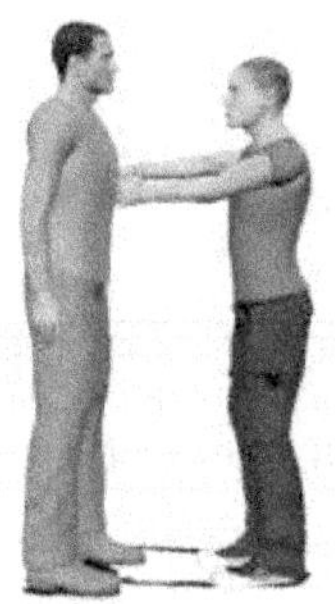

Lock the hands with the rear hand.

Step forward (going with) into a horse and executing a ridgehand to the groin.

Inward block raking the nose.

However, the inward block rake to the nose takes time, and does not feed the flow. To do it you have to stop the ridge hand, lift the hand, chop the hand. That's an awful lot to do and expect the attacker to do nothing, especially after he's been clocked in the peanuts.

Cup ear and chop neck.

Chop neck and ear slap is too much. You only need one. Hitting with both sides of the body tends to put energy down both sides of the body. You can summon up more energy by pushing the energy down one side of the body.

Chapter Thirty
Hidden Sword B

Defense for two handed lapel pull.

Slightly better as you are now using one side of the body. The push down on the arms is much better, but then you have the same excessive back and forth motion with the chop.

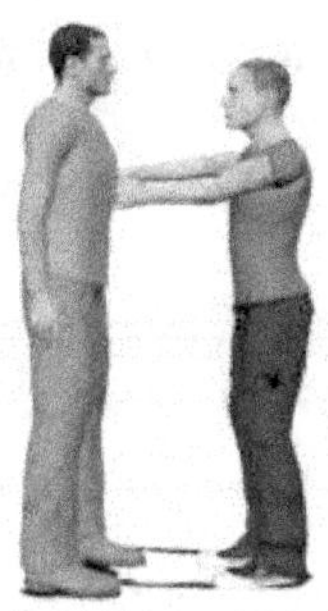
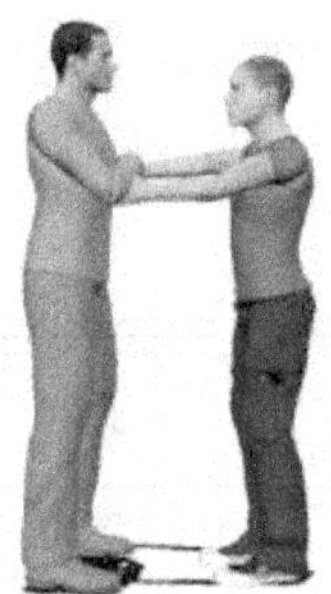

Lock hands with rear hand as you step into a horse.

Step forward (going with) into a horse and executing a ridgehand to the groin.

Push both hands straight down with the locking hand and chop the neck with the forward hand.

Might be better, after the ridgehand, to just push up on the arm and create an armbar/elbow roll kind of technique.

Do people still use lapels? Maybe this should be adapted to a two handed push? just thinking out loud, but...?

Chapter Thirty-One
Hand of the Dragon A

Defense for throat grab.

This is a classic technique. I've seen it in virtually every martial art I have ever seen.

It does takes finesse, and let me make apologies before we continue. I remember the technique being easier to work than I have depicted here. Perhaps my notes were bad, if not my memory. That said, my recommendations are below.

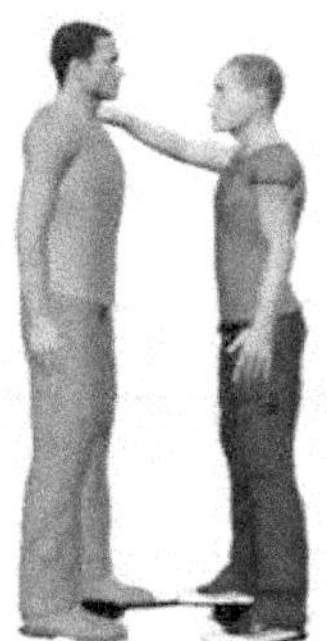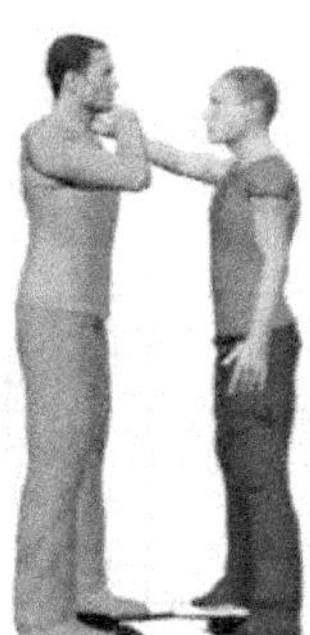

Reach over hand and grasp, inserting your thumb under his thumb.

This should be done on both sides, and with both hands, turning the hands clockwise or counterclockwise. That is the matrix viewpoint. It takes into account all potentials, and gives a total of four basic wrist twist techniques. That will really educate the beginner.

Step back and twist.

Pull attacker out.

Stomp to the midsection.

Now, it would be easier to pull back and keep the elbow straight, armbar style, rather than do a crank and then a pull to an armbar.

Also, I sort of recall doing this technique with a snap kick to the midsection and not a thrust. Instead of me recommending one over the other, however, let me just say that you should practice both, and be able to choose which one you want to do. It's the only way to be sure. Grin.

Chapter Thirty-Two
Doors of the Shrine

Front bear hug, arms pinned.

Another good technique. Guy thinks he's got you trapped, so you tweak his manhood, bash his manhood, open up the distance, and knock the stuffings out of him.

Twist hands into groin with thumbs extended.

Now, the problem with this is that it should be a full groin grab. SQUEEZE! But that's a hard thing to sell a mother that her little girl should, uh, 'handle' another student. So they 'tweak' with the thumbs. So...cool. We go with tweak.

Bring knee to groin.

Step forward slightly and push throat with chop hand.

Knee is great, and opening distance is great. Get him to jerk back from the groin, then take advantage of his body motion to move in and increase distance and set him up.

I do wonder, though. A push to the throat is right, but if you can get the room a full on chop is better. Still, the scenario here works.

Punch to the solar plexus.

I'd like something better, but I don't know what. A punch seems pretty light after the previous damage, and the distance may not be right yet. But, still, you're increasing distance.

Maybe some kind of throw? I'll let you work on that one.

Chapter Thirty-Three
Releasing the Vice A

Escape from a headlock.
Should see it coming, but it is real, got to start somewhere.

Step forward with outside leg and hammerfist to groin and hammerfist to far kidney.

I've been in headlocks that were really tough, but this technique seems to work. There are better solutions, but this is excellent for a beginner. Gets him used to the idea that there are simple solutions to most problems.

Cross out and set.

Chapter Thirty-Four
Releasing the Vice B

Escape from a headlock.

This is probably better than the previous. Should go for a full grab in real life, however. Crushing will hurt more than a strike, in many cases.

Grab forearm, step back with the inside leg into kneeling position and ridgehand to the groin.

Cross out and set.

Chapter Thirty-Five
Releasing the Vice C

Escape from a headlock.

Manipulating a whole body by pressing on the frenum really works. The only problem is being flexible enough to reach over and grab. Still this is good for an introduction to the ease of pressure points.

Reach over the head with the inside hand and place flat fingers under frenum (nose).

Lift head by the frenum.

Pivot into front stance as you execute a palm thrust to throat with the other hand.

Cross out and set.

A little tight for a front stance, the bodies get a little awkward. Maybe a claw to the throat? Maybe something else?

Chapter Thirty-Six
Descending Arrow A

Two-handed choke from rear.

I was going through various systems, cross checking my notes on the way I was originally taught, and this technique has apparently been changed. I assume because it makes no sense to have somebody choking from the back with perfect straight hands. It is now taught, in some systems, as a single hand shoulder grab from the rear. Works both ways, and i am glad to see that people are looking at this stuff and thinking about it.

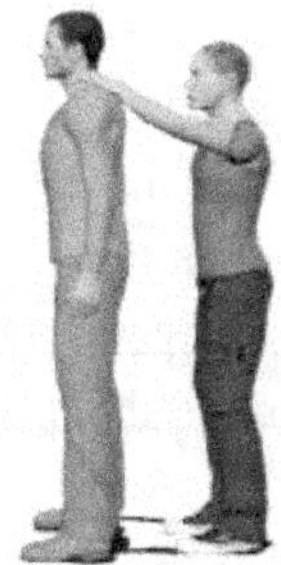

Step forward and turn, slashing chop across the neck.

The turn and slash works. Works well. A guy once did it to me, I had gone to classical karate, and we were fooling around, and his turn and slash negated my proud classical karate methods. Nice.

Punch to the head.

Punch to the head.

And, I have nothing against the punch and punch, except that it might be better to punch the body, then the head. that would make the blocks go up and down, and leave openings after each strike and natural body reaction to getting struck on the part of the attacker.

Good technique, and better when used on the shoulder grab.

Cross out and set.

Chapter Thirty-Seven
Descending Arrow B

Two-handed choke from rear.

I have a problem with this technique. You kick, which starts the motion one way, then you bring the foot forward, another direction, which you might get away with, but then you step in an entirely different direction.

Heck, do the kick, then set the foot down behind yourself, jam the guy as you turn, use the elbows if you are close, instead of a chop, and it would work.

But don't go in three directions and expect it to work. It screws up the CBM, not to mention the tactics and strategy.

Right kick to groin.

Right foot steps across and turn, hitting arms with left arm and chopping neck with left hand.

Right punch to face.

Again, after chopping high, punch low. Set him up.

Chapter Thirty-Eight
Sharpening the Blade B

Defense for a lapel grab with one hand.

Excellent technique. Simple, and the body alignment is right. The horse stance works here.

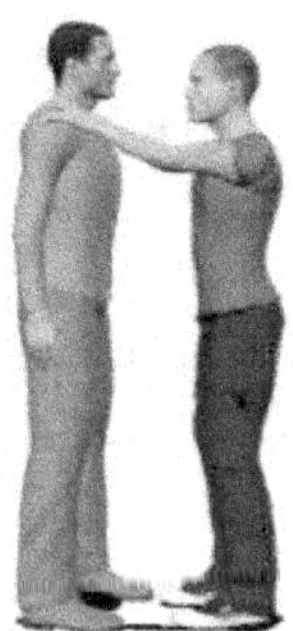 

Step back as you circle the arm and grab.

Pull him as you execute a palm strike with the other hand.

Chapter Thirty-Nine
Capturing Paws B

Bear hug with arms pinned.

I have some problems with this one.

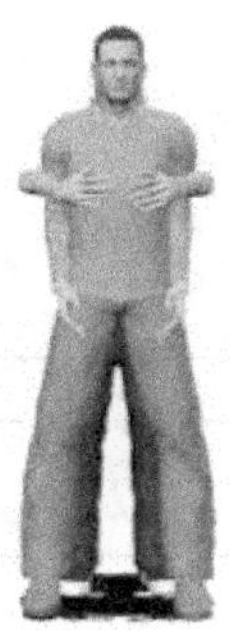 

Step to side hammerfist to groin.

Starts out fine. A good weight drop into a horse stance will unbalance the attacker and may open up the groin area. Not bad.

Claw groin as you assume a cat stance.

Step behind into horse as you elbow smash to chin and hammerfist to groin.

But now you are trying to walk around somebody, somebody who's arm gets in the way, who's leg gets in the way. It can work, and maybe it should be here because it is a trial for the student. But, quite honestly, even when struck in the groin, I don't think somebody is going to wait around and let you do this technique.

Chapter Forty
Tangled Wings B

Escape from Full Nelson.
Yikes.

Step out and double back knuckle to temples.
Weak. Backfists don't have a lot of power. Might work for some people.

Slip downward out of hold.
I've tried this, and it didn't work. The guy I was working with just held on. Still, this low stance has a LOT of power.
Cat stance to side as you claw the groin.
We run into the same problem we ran into last technique. The awkwardness of this close in work is just not beginner quality, and there tends to be a bit of the poser here.

Step behind to horse stance as you execute an elbow to the chin and a hammerfist to the groin.

Interestingly, in cross checking this technique, I didn't find it anywhere. Perhaps some schools have dropped it out, possibly because of the unworkability I have pointed out here.

Chapter Forty-One
Chopping Bamboo B

Shoulders grabbed from each side.

I always have difficulty with two man self defenses. Fighting two men at the same time splits the intention, so I almost always stay away from the techniques in Kenpo.

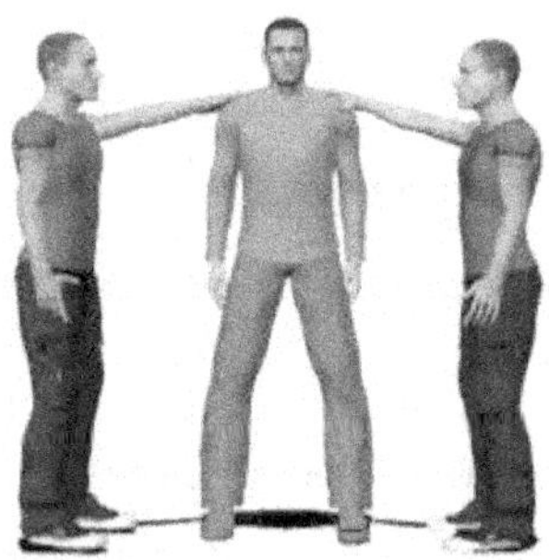

Step slightly forward with right foot as you chop neck of opponent on right.

The above objection noted, what is the man on your left going to do while you are chopping?

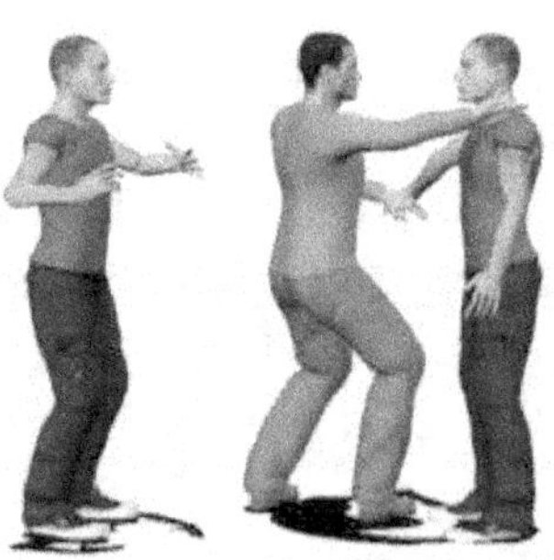

Cross step with right foot, pivot and slash eyes of opponent on left with left claw.

Chop neck of opponent on left with right hand.

Step away with left foot as you block punch with right inward block.
Right snap kick to opponent on right groin.

Right rear kick to midsection of opponent on left.
Cross out and set.

I had a LOT of trouble with distances in this technique. I have seen high ranking Kenpoists make it work, but I have still not been impressed. There are just easier and more efficient ways of handling a situation like this.

Purple Belt Techniques

chapter forty two
Ram's head

Defense for right overhead smash.

Yikes! We start out fine. Good alignment to the high block, good distance for...a punch! But it is too far away for an elbow strike! And when you do the outward block, later in the form, you are too close for that and have to back up!

Step forward with the left foot into a horse stance as you execute a left high block.

Right elbow strike to ribs.

The above noted, I do like the elbow strike. And maybe even two of them. After all, if you get away with one, nothing wrong with giving him another!

Left elbow strike to ribs.

Left outward block and hook arm.

I also have a problem with the wrap. You are that close, in his face, and he is just going to sit there and let you wrap his arm? And then half punch his throat? And, to complicate the matter, you are jerking your left arm inwards, to the right, and trying to punch with the right arm at the same time. This tend sot cross the body, to counter twist it. Yes, it can be made to work, especially if the attacker is compliant. But what attacker is going to be compliant?

Right half fist to throat.

So what is the solution? I would prefer high block, elbow, elbow, maybe a knee and a takedown. That would keep the closing of distances in the right sequence. You might have to get creative with the takedown, however.

technique 43
Cocking the Bow

Defense against forward rushing right overhead smash.

The first part of this technique is great. Simple block, straight shot to chin. Then it falls apart.

Step back with the right foot to a horse stance as you execute a left high block.

Pivot into a left bow stance as you execute a palm thrust to the chin.

Pivot to the right into a right bow stance as you execute a left chop to the throat.

Why would you turn your weight OUT of the technique? This TOTALLY takes the power out of the strike and unaligns the body.

Further, wouldn't the defender grab his throat, or at least cover it, after being struck their once?

technique 44
Sacred Chopsticks

Defense for a right kick.

The thing is, this technique works. Going into a kneeling stance stops the defender from leaning forward (as in a front stance). However, kicking from the kneeling position is slow. Might be good for training and body strength.

Drop to kneeling stance with left foot forward as you execute a Crossed wrist block with the left hand on top.

Grab the heel with the right hand and push the toes with the right hand and twist the foot, and leg, and whole body.

Right snap kick to the groin while opponent is turned away.

Double palm thrust to kidney.

It is better to just slap the foot to the side, the kick between the legs works just as well.

Right heel thrust to kidney.

Cross out and set.

I don't think this technique is perfect, but it is good, and the next progression afterwards should be to take the ankle twist into a takedown. I always like a good takedown, and if you actually are twisting the joint, it messes with the idea of collapsing distance to a takedown, because it goes back out to a kick. Still, that might happen in a fight if somebody falls out of the technique.

technique 45
Eagle's Grasp

Grab with right hand to left shoulder, attacker facing same direction as defender.

I like the first chop. Simple and to the point. But a guy probably wouldn't keep hanging on to your shoulder if you chopped him in the throat. But, if he did, I can even see the arm wrap.

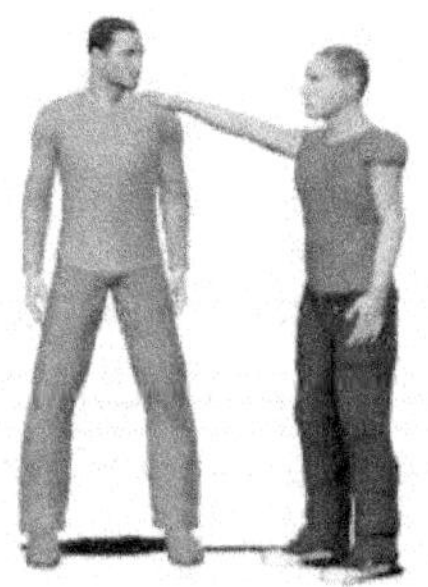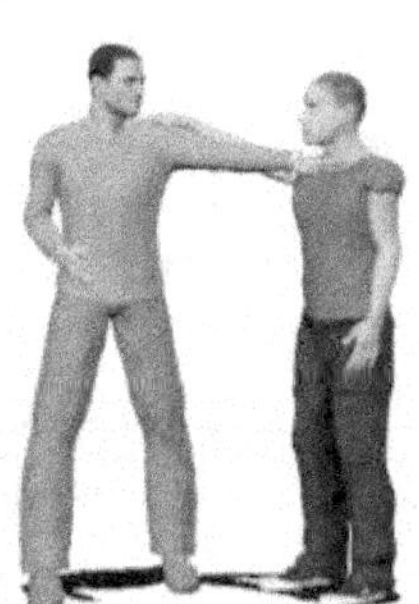

Right hand locks the grab hand.
Slight step forward with right foot and chop to neck with left hand.

Step back as you circle the left hand and wrap/lock the attacker's arm.
Reverse circle of the left arm and back knuckle to the back of the attacker's head.

VERY hard to break an elbow with an arm wrap, even if the opponent lets you do it. But, the back knuckle to the back of the head, that's a weak strike to a hard skull. Not a good thing.

Chop to neck with left hand.

But that chop. It is good. Except that if you knuckled the back of his head he might have lowered his chin and closed the door.

Cross out and set.

So I like some parts of this technique. I say do the chop, then just punch the sucker. Or, if you are advancing the technique, step behind or in front of him and trip one way or the other.

technique 46
Charging Bull D

Defense for a frontal rush (single/double leg takedown).

One of the most effective techniques if someone grabs you. But it isn't that effective before they grab you. Like so many Kenpo techniques, it's a dream.

Cross step behind your foot and pivot as you strike the neck with a chop.

Chop the neck again.

Side (knife) kick to the head.

Rework this technique so you can ground your weight when they rush, then chop them in the back of the neck. Guaranteed, only one chop is going to be necessary. BUT, it's nice to tack on a grab art after that chop. Which brings us to the next technique, which is MUCH better.

technique 47
Charging Bull E

Defense for a frontal rush (single/double leg takedown).
He thinks he's got you, and you simply knock him out with a chop.
And, yes. This will result in an easy knock out.

Cross step behind your foot and pivot as you strike the neck with a chop.

Circle arm to trap attacker's arm.
I don't know about the circle of the arm. Hard to do and not necessary.

Knee to face.
Back to horse and hammerfist to neck.
But the knee and the hammer...they are nothing but joy!

technique 48
Crouching Cat

Warding a right punch from the left side.

Excellent technique. He goes high, you go low. He thinks about the groin, you poke his eyes. Grabbing sets up takedowns and other things. No complaints on this technique.

Jump left to cat stance as you execute an upwards beak.

Snap kick to the groin.
Finger jab to the eyes.

Grab shoulder and pull attacker in and execute a palm up spear to the throat.

Cross out and set.

technique 49
Chinese Servant

Right Punch from left side.

Though I am not fond of the windshield wiper block, it works. I can't make it work, but I have had people who have made it work on me, and it was devastating. I guess I just need more practice.

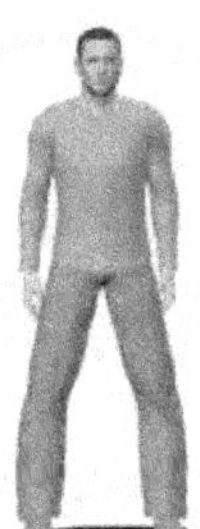  

Move into opponent with right cross palm guiding block.

Follow with a left rising back hand parry (this is sometimes called a windshield block).

Horse stance with left elbow spike to armpit.

Left hand rakes down, pulling the right arm while palm thrust to face.

So I do like this technique. Especially the end, where you pull and palm. Really takes advantage of correct body alignment.

technique 50
Twisted Wing B

Escape from an armlock.

This technique assumes a certain grab, which is actually not likely to happen. One will usually grab with two hands, or a second hand to the shoulder, and so on.

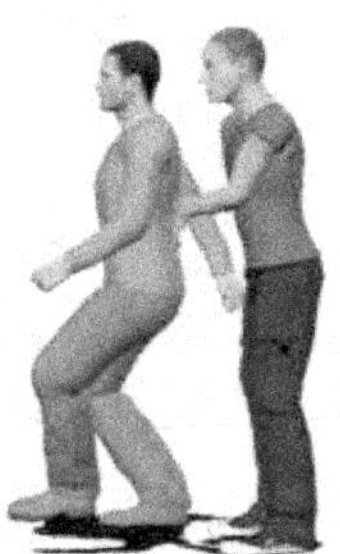

Cross step and hammer groin.
Still, if you do manage the first move, the rest will work.

Pivot and punch the face with the other hand.

It's not bad, just sort of weak in the beginning. Perhaps good for a beginner who knows no better.

I may have set this up with the wrong hand, but it shouldn't matter. Works with either hand. That's a good thing.

technique 51
Twisted Wing C

Escape from an armlock.

This isn't bad. A good elbow to the chops may shock the fellow long enough to step out of the lock.

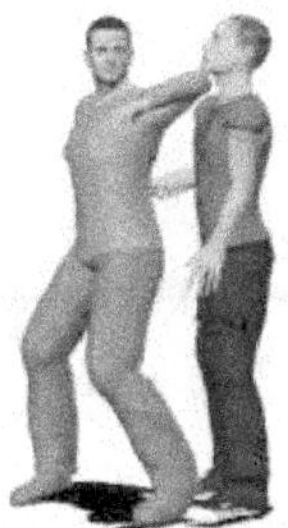

Step to the rear and elbow strike to Attacker's head.

Step forward and turn under the arm.
Pull so the arm straightens and attacker has to bend.

Chicken kick.

I do think there are better kicks than the chicken kick.

Maybe do a shuffle kick, or some kind of power kick, then save the chicken kick for advanced work.

One of the weakness of Kenpo is giving an advanced technique, and the chicken kick is advanced, before the bread and butter kicks have been drilled to power and perfection.

technique 52
Broken Hourglass

Defense for a cross the body grab to the shoulder.

The locking hand is a bit weak. Better to do the block and then use the locking hand to catch and turn. Still, I wouldn't curse anybody if they stayed with the locking hand. It does help the beginner set up an entry.

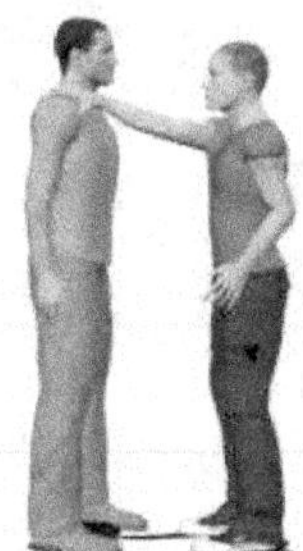 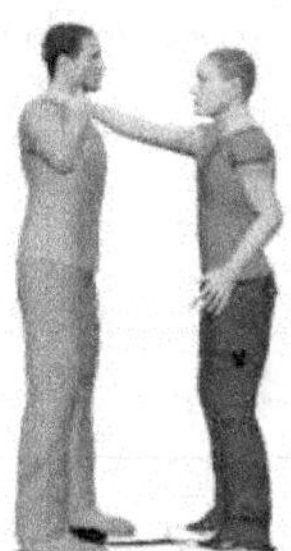

Lock the attacker's hand.

Step forward and execute an inward block
Push the arm over to make an armbar.

Elbow spike to the head.

Elbow spike to the spine.

I especially like the education involved in the spikes. It is one of the few kenpo techniques that draws upon the horse stance's ability to create an effective connection with the ground.

technique 53
Sacred Spike

Defense for right knee attack.

It just doesn't make sense that you would lower yourself. It immobilizes you and puts you under the weight of his attack.

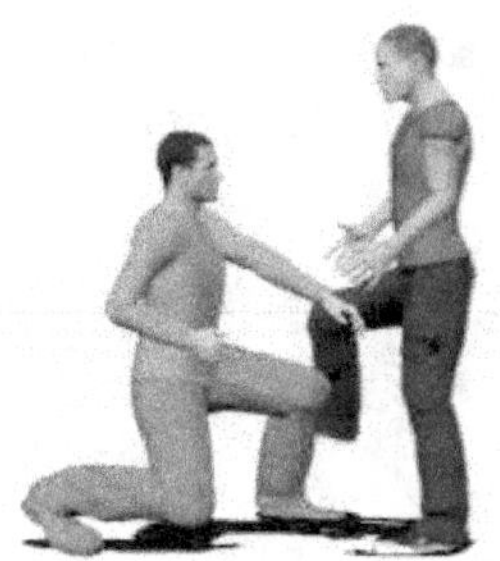 

Step back with right leg to kneeling stance.

Circle left arm over and down to push knee out.

Left elbow strike to groin.

Also, perhaps it is my memory, or my notes, but this is awkward and weak. Admitted, my notes could be a mistake, but any type of elbow strike is going to be awkward in this position, regardless of my memory.

I like dropping the weight on the knee, I do that, but from a stance. So if you changed the stance and did a different strike, then maybe.

Also, it is harder to get away if you have to lift yourself up from a kneeling stance.

For the above reasons I just don't recommend this technique.

technique 54
Flashing Thong

Defense for a two punches.

I had trouble defining this technique. My notes weren't totally clear, and the technique had disappeared from some of the kenpo systems i examined, and when I did find it in other places, it seemed to be very altered from what I had. At any rate, the first two blocks are great. And I like the kick, though if the attacker is punching then you should punch, or close distance for a knee or elbow, or back up for a kick. Changing distances like this in a fight is a strategy, but you have to be careful

Inward block, move into cat stance, outward block.

I found this as one punch and outward block in some places, but I have it written down as two punches. Oh well.

Snap kick to groin. Knife edge to knee.

Rear kick to chest.

One thing I don't like in this technique is the three kicks. Difficult to get the kicks off like this because you have to turn the body. First two, yes, and maybe that gives you time for the third.

But three kicks like this might work for an advanced student, but it is a weakness to have a beginning student do this. I always believe that a student should drill those feet for a couple of years before trying this type of defense.

Also, I've said it before and I'll say it again, knife edges are not good kicks. A foot stomp, such as I have indicated, would work MUCH better. But it would cut speed down a bit, and then the third kick wouldn't work.

About the Author

Al Case walked into his first martial arts school in 1967. During the Gold Age of Martial Arts he studied such arts as Aikido, Wing Chun, Ton Toi Northern Shaolin, Fut Ga Southern Shaolin, Weapons, Tai Chi Chuan, Pa Kua Chang, and others.

In 1981 he began writing for the martial arts magazines, including Inside Karate, Inside Kung Fu, Black Belt, Masters and Styles, and more.

In 1991 he was asked to write his own column in Inside Karate.

Beginning in 2001 he completed the basic studies of Matrixing, a logic approach to the Martial Arts he had been working on for over 30 years.

2011 he was heavily immersed in creating Neutronics, the science behind the science of Matrixing.

Currently he resides at Monkeyland, a location in Southern California where plans to build a martial arts temple are underway.

Interested martial artists can avail themselves of his research into Matrixing at MonsterMartialArts.com.

THE 'MATRIXING KENPO KARATE' JOURNEY!

The most incredible analysis of Kenpo Karate in the world.
In depth Matrixing of over 150 Kenpo techniques.
New ways of doing Kenpo forms.
New ways of teaching and structuring classes.
A COMPLETE REWORK OF ONE OF THE MOST
IMPORTANT MARTIAL ARTS SYSTEMS IN THE WORLD!

Over 40,000 words
Nearly 400 pages
Over 800 graphics

Only possible through…

the logic of Matrixing!

Pan Gai Noon (half hard/half soft) is a style of Chinese Kung Fu originally taught about 1900.

It was taught by a street hawker named Shu Shi Wa, and may have had roots in the Temple Gung Fu of the times.

It eventually was transformed into a style of Karate called Uechi Ryu.

The style therefore links Karate to Kung Fu, which makes it one of the more important martial arts, historically and technically speaking.

In this volume the art of Pan Gai Noon has been resurrected through the logic of Matrixing.

The first two forms, plus drills and techniques, are presented, making this a valuable addition to any martial artist's library.

Available on the internet

Kang Duk Won Korean Karate, the one Karate that resulted in the development of the five Korean systems which later became Taekwondo.

This is a pure form of Karate from before the Funakoshi and Japanese influence.

It was chosen by the Imperial bodyguards of three different nations, Okinawa, Korea, and Japan.

Available on the internet

Kwon Bup is a form of American Karate developed by Sensei Robert Babich of the Kang Duk Won. It is linear and powerful, and the ultimate expression of the only American to ever do the 'One Finger Trick.'

Sensei Babich could thrust a finger through a board and not break it, but leave a hole.

This is his art, his forms and techniques, his method of bringing Karate to the highest stage.

Available on the internet

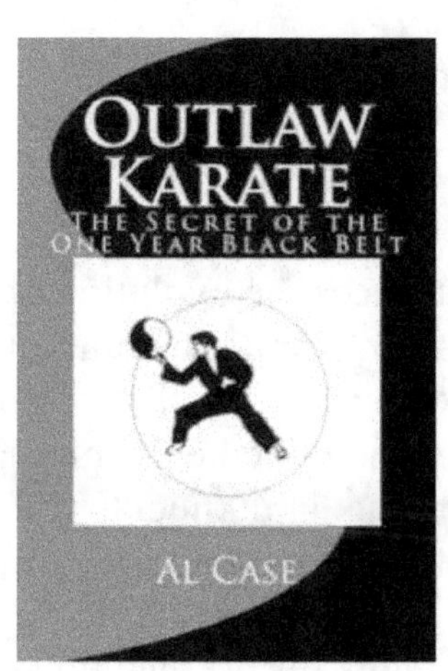

Outlaw Karate is the synthesis of two methods of Karate, Kang Duk Won (House for Espousing Virtue), and Kwon Bup (The Fist Method).

These arts were stripped of duplicate movements and poser techniques, then boiled down to six easy to learn (and thus easy to use) forms.

The result was a form of Karate that could be taught in less than one year, while keeping the original power of Karate, and even enhancing it.

This art set the stage for breakthroughs in the Martial Science of Matrixing.

Any karate student wishing to learn an extremely powerful form of Karate, and to delve into the history of Matrixing, should definitely look into Outlaw Karate.

Available on the internet

Matrixing is a form of logic.

While it can be used in any endeavor, it is specific to the Martial Arts.

Buddha Crane Karate is a very pivotal Martial Art as it was created just as the author was figuring out the logic of Matrixing.

In this book you get to see the exact thought process that is Matrixing at work; you will see the principles which would later crop up in his courses on Matrixing.

In addition, Buddha Crane is an entire Martial Art, built from the ground up. Thus you get to see exactly, how and why an art takes form. This will definitely enlighten any who wish to inspect their own martial art and truly understand what they are seeing.

Available on the internet

The book that traces the evolution of internal power from Karate to Gung Fu.

There are three manuals in this volume, and they are designed to take the martial arts student from the hard knuckles of karate to the soft, internal practices of Gung Fu.

This book contains forms, techniques, training drills, and the theory necessary to help a student evolve quickly and natural.

Available on the internet

The Most Important Martial Arts Breakthrough in History

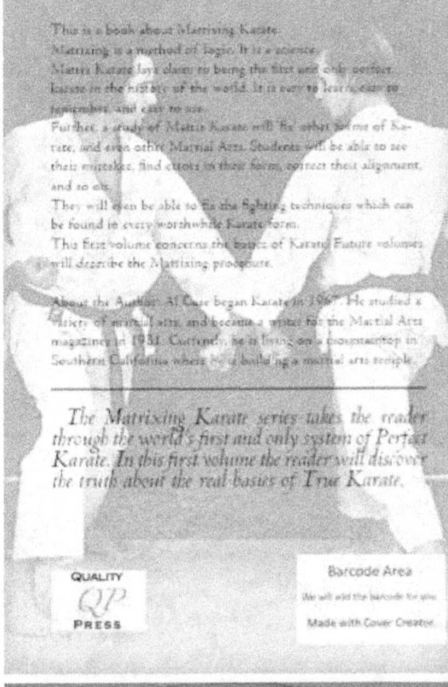

The Mysteries of the Martial Arts Resolved Through Matrixing

MATRIXING KARATE
Available on the internet

There are companion DVDs to many of these books, and you can find them at:

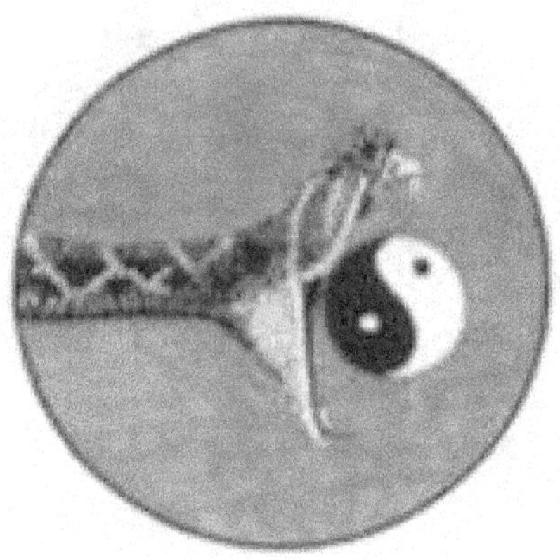

MonsterMartialArts.com

Did you know...

Al Case has written over forty novels?
Many of them have martial arts sub themes.
Many of these novels are available on the internet.
Or simply go to:

<u>AlCaseBooks.com</u>